Celebrating Beginnings and Endings

Celebrating Beginnings and Endings

Mark the Moment Book 1

Text and Illustrations by Paula Pugh

Sound Wisdom Press
Langley, WA

Celebrating Beginnings and Endings

S Sound Wisdom Press
Langley, WA

Book design by Robin Simonds, Beagle Bay, Inc.

ISBN: 978-0-9837043-2-4
LCCN: 2011909365

First Edition
Printed in China
16 15 14 13 12   1 2 3 4 5 6 7 8 9

Dedication

To my late father-in-law, Allen C. Blume

Foreword

Life so often seems to hurry us along. There is so much to do in a day, and one life event after another occurs with very little time to reflect on the significance of something before the next thing happens. There are so many people to interact with—from emails to passersby to work or community colleagues, to those we love. The hours zip along, and then the days become weeks, and the seasons become years. Paula Pugh has made great use of this passage of time by studying how to mark the moments of life, designing simple ways to stop and call forward the significance of life events and experiences. In her practical and creative fashion she has collected ideas, tools, and practices that we can learn from her and do ourselves.

Through years of doing it herself Paula has captured the essence of what makes something memorable. In this book she models the three essentials for holding ceremonies in our own families, communities, and organizations. She understands the need to:

Create a physical environment that supports what you want to have happen:

A circle, a center, appropriate levels of privacy and quiet, and touches of beauty.

Slow down the interactions: By calling people to listen and speak with attention and intention, to name what is going on, and invite (not demand) participation.

Make stories: Speak in story as much as possible during the moment, and help people remember by making a story out of what happened.

With these essentials in mind, Paula provides a recipe for celebrations that can be adapted with great variety and application. I know her recipe works because I've been privileged to participate in moments she's designed, and for a number of years we have been colleagues learning from each other.

In her section on "Learning to Mark the Moment," Paula lays out the tools and practicalities for these essentials, and I'd like to speak of each aspect a little more in depth.

Creating a physical environment.

How we set the chairs sets the expectations for what is about to happen. Chairs in rows create an expectation of audience, of being receivers of information or entertainment with little or no input. Chairs in a circle create an invitation to participate, being deliverers of information and entertainment with shared input.

The circle needs a center: a place in the middle that is decorated to represent the "why" people are gathered. Paula gives many fine examples throughout her stories: baby things at a baby shower, mementoes and photos at a family reunion, flowers at a garden party. The reason behind this is ancient: for thousands of years people have learned to be in circle by gathering around cook fires and telling each other stories and passing along bits of needed information that helped insure survival, developed the growth of community, and encouraged a sense of belonging. We still want these things from each other: help, connection, and belonging.

When we sit in circles today our gaze naturally rests in the center, then looks at who is speaking, and back to the center. Something needs to be placed there that is pleasant to look at and supports the mood of the moment. Once you understand what the center is for, making one is great fun—and it can be fancy or simple. And when a conversation starts to shift to celebration, spontaneously establishing a center, like sitting on the beach and making a design of clam shells, or sitting in the woods and making a design of pine cones or sitting in a restaurant and making a pinwheel of spoons, helps people feel more present.

Once people are present, the circle needs a host. Paula talks about the recipe for celebration in this book and that's a great metaphor for who *you* are: you are the host. And hosting a circle is like hosting a dinner party: you cook, you set the space, you create ambience, and serve the food—and then you partake of the meal along with everyone else. In the circle, you set intention, you invite folks to gather, you offer the pattern of interaction, and then you join in—helping people feel comfortable and contributing your own stories.

Slowing down the interactions

Creating a circle and a center automatically begins to relax the pace of interaction. People stop *going* somewhere, and start *being* somewhere. We come together. Sometimes we try to interact at the same pace as the machinery we've developed. "Hey . . . Hi . . . Fine . . . Bye . . . Yeah, lunch soon . . . ." When we talk in text messages and abbreviations we manage to communicate—but not at depth. Paula puts much emphasis here about the depth of conversation and how meaningful depth is. Depth doesn't necessarily mean serious: it means choosing to share what has relevance to the moment and listening carefully to each other so that people can connect in a heart-based way.

When I am invited to a celebration, there is one question I ask myself: how do I want to contribute to the well being of the group? Sometimes I know immediately, and sometimes I don't know until I'm sitting with the group and waiting for my turn to speak. What I do know is that this question helps me prepare myself to slow down and be present. My friend, cultural anthropologist, Angeles Arrien, says it this way, "Show up. Pay attention. Follow what has heart and meaning." As you read Paula's stories, you'll see that is what she is coaching all of us to do.

Making stories

Words are how we think: stories are how we link. Stories are how we link one life experience to the next—so that we can learn from them, savor them, and share our memories with each other. Paula understands the power of story in all her work. She doesn't create celebrations that pass along data and information: she creates time and space for people to share stories because stories stay with us for the long haul. Stories are a kind of map we provide each other: here's how I did it, here's what I learned, here's what I wish I'd known. We don't expect that one another's experience will be exactly the same, but we do know that stories help.

As you become someone who is called on to provide meaningful moments in your family or friendship groups, you will realize that people are actually asking you to help them tell and listen to stories. A baby shower is not a gathering where the mother-to-be wants statistics on the average length of labor; it's a gathering where she wants a story because story connects her to the experience of other mothers and women in the room.

Stories occur in response to a questioning invitation: tell us a story about the most meaningful moment during: your wedding / childbirth / moving to a new job / retirement / etc. Or, what's the funniest thing that ever happened to you when. . . .

Stories are the treasures that will come from marking the moments in your life. I have loved reading Paula's stories—and am excited that she has ways to collect more stories from readers. *Celebrating Beginnings and Endings* is a movement back to remembering how much pleasure people can have in each other's company, with the techno-toys turned off, and the basic of social space reactivated between us. Enjoy. Join. And celebrate.

Christina Baldwin is the author of *The Circle Way, Calling the Circle, Storycatcher,* and other titles. The fullness of her work is available at www.peerspirit.com.

Contents

■

Acknowledgements

Grateful thanks to:

Dr. Christiane Northrup, who provided me the inspiration that led to this project.

Christina Baldwin and Ann Linnea of Peerspirit who encouraged me to take their training.

Christine Nyberg and Kimberly Cerra of CK Websites for help in designing the www.mark-the-moment.com website and the Sound Wisdom logo.

Jacqueline Church Simonds and Robin Simonds of Beagle Bay, Inc, who have patiently ushered me through the process of publishing.

BJ Elliot and Yvonne Billera, who read the very first rough drafts.

The women who have taken my classes and retreats and shared their stories.

My Quarterly Quartet writing group, for the constant encouragement.

My family for their patience and support, allowing me to "practice" on them with hardly ever a complaint.

All of who you have allowed me to use your stories. You are the core of this work and an inspiration for the rest of us to create meaningful moments.

Celebrating Beginnings and Endings

Introduction

I meet on a regular basis with my friend, Victor. He lives next door in a nursing home, as he is 103 years old and needs extra help these days. His eyesight is poor with macular degeneration taking over, yet his hearing and his mind are keen. I have spent several months visiting with him on a weekly basis—health permitting—and reading this manuscript to him. He is a scientist, author of fourteen books and a kind man. After working together for a couple of months, Victor said to me, "This is a book about love."

I sat back and thought about it for a while and I had to agree with him. This *is* a book about love. *Celebrating Beginnings and Endings* explains and models how to create circles of love. It shows how to set the stage when you want to connect with people concerning important "starts" in life: births, adoption, graduation, weddings and religious ceremonies. Transitions help define beginnings and endings in the middle years when life is in flux: divorce, coming of age, taking on a new role, moving or empty nest syndrome. Endings touch on terminal illness, miscarriage and death of people

3

as well as pets. When you can see love in these passages, you—and those around you—will be changed from a passive participant to an active leader, allowing for a transformation from mundane to magical. With each person taking a role in promoting and acting in these circles of love, the world will slowly move into a place of caring, support and peace. It's worth the effort to learn how to do this.

Join me as we explore the many ways people have added this ingredient of love into their lives. *Celebrating Beginnings and Endings* takes us to a place of learning to express our appreciation for others. Be enriched by the adventure.

At a certain age, a person may feel that she wants more in and from life. Relationships seem shallow. Parties lack vitality. Life's milestones are deliberately ignored. If these feelings nag at your soul—that deep place inside of you where truth resides— then you're ready for *Celebrating Beginnings and Endings*. I didn't know it, but my life would take on a new and dynamic course when I was able to open up and have the courage to follow the road laid out in front of and for me. That feeling of discontentment led me out of my status quo and onto a voyage of discovery that would forever change the course of my life and those around me.

Celebrating Beginnings and Endings is the result of the desire to share how to create heartfelt occasions. You will be opening up a new realm of meeting life at a different level by creating a place to tell people how you appreciate them, to help them through trauma, and to celebrate emotional milestones. As exhilarating as skydiving or skiing might be, the opportunity to tell a person how you value them, or support a friend during a crisis, can offer a buzz that can cause goose bumps. As you read this book, you will be called to be a guide to a new reality for your community, family and friends. Be prepared to be inspired by the many stories of what people have already done. When you are ready to move into action, the recipe and tools presented later will assist you on your journey of creating a special gathering.

Put on your magical dancing shoes and move into the world of low-cost and enchanting celebrations. You are the creator of your own fate, and *Celebrating Beginnings and Endings* will assist and encourage you to take charge to make a new course for your world.

You now set in motion a journey of freshening your senses by taking the time to add meaning and vitality to unique events, which are sprinkled throughout life. Instinctively you recognize these milestones, but often don't know how to pay tribute to them. *Celebrating Beginnings and Endings* acts as your guide to unlock the deep potential and magic available to all who desire to add this extra dimension to meaningful moments.

Here is the first recipe to begin this journey of discovery:

Mark the Moment

1 dose of Courage
1 pinch of Creativity
Stir in some Trust
Sift in lots of
    Encouragement

You now have the makings for a delicious celebration, ready for any occasion. In the following pages you will

- Learn why it is important to mark these moments
- Find out how to create celebrations using the easily accessible recipe
- Discover tools to help make the gatherings happen
- Read stories of what people have already done to enhance their experiences

Read this story example to whet your appetite and encourage your curiosity:

Introduction

In 1962, I was a seventeen-year-old girl wearing saddle shoes with my socks rolled down, Peter Pan-style blouses with plaid pleated skirts, and attending a large high school near San Francisco. As my senior year approached, four of my friends and I realized that our class schedules were arranged so that we wouldn't be seeing each other as often as we had planned. That wouldn't work for us. We wanted and needed to stay connected. In order to bridge that gap, we decided to initiate a group journal. This would allow us to stay in touch on a daily basis. The plan was for one girl to take the spiral-bound notebook to her First Period class. No one would even realize that she was writing in a journal because it looked like she was taking notes. When the bell rang for the classes to change, she passed off the notebook to the second girl. The notebook went into five classrooms every day.

Karen and Terry had been friends since they were three years old. Joanne was in Ceiny's sixth grade class. I didn't come into the friend-scene until the eighth grade. Our parents all knew each other. Our roots were tangled and deep.

By the end of the year, we filled five notebooks with writings of school activities: football games, yearbook issues, school newspaper plans and political happenings: the Cuban Missile crisis, Jacqueline Kennedy, the first black student to enter the University of Mississippi (though under guard), who's going with whom to the prom, who's going steady this week, who broke up, philosophical musings inspired from our

English class readings, "West Side Story" as the best movie, the first Beatles album, Marilyn Monroe dying, and all that passed through our collective minds that year.

We moved out into the world in different directions after graduation—we became teachers, a lawyer, wives and mothers. We moved to different states: California, Minnesota, Washington, Utah. Some had children, some didn't. Some married, some didn't. Several lived near each other and kept in close touch, and I lived far away. Our lives were diverse, but our hearts were still connected because of the year of writing and shared growing-up history.

Forty years later we learned that Karen was dying of lung cancer in Utah. One of our own was going to leave us permanently, and she was far too young. The other four of us reconnected on email with the news and pondered what we could do for our friend. We finally decided that showing up was the best we could offer. We all flew to Salt Lake City and drove to the small town where Karen was living. Now, going to visit a dying friend whom you haven't seen in many years isn't for the faint of heart, yet we were on a mission to spend time with our friend, and that gave us the courage to do what we needed and wanted to do. We could also lean on each other during this challenging time.

As we parked by her house, we saw that her single-wide mobile home was neat and tidy. A lovely handmade quilt hung on the wall highlighting significant events in her life. Two of Karen's four children stayed with us the entire time, listening to the stories about their mom, and learning about who she was as a young woman. With the help of three of the journals, we laughed, cried, remembered who we were when we were seventeen, and we delighted in re-establishing relationships.

I brought along wisdom doll making kits—bits of silk fabric, feathers, glittery pipe cleaners, ribbon, thread and needles used to create a small whimsical being to help keep our fantasies alive. This was a quiet activity in which we could all participate. Traditional working with the hands, as the conversation flowed and more stories emerged, added a timeless quality to the weekend.

The gathering was in May, and Karen died in September. Each year after her death, we send a bouquet of sunflowers to Karen's parents on her birthday. The wish to remain connected with the family and honor Karen is strong.

This simple story shows how we figured out how to seize the opportunity, move into action, show up to honor our friend, and tap into the rich shared history of the group. It was the best thing we could have done for her. As it turns out, it was probably the best thing we could have done for ourselves as part of processing her loss in our lives. During our visit, Karen still felt physically well enough to participate and enjoy our presence. The fact that her children were around and could also share the stories about their mother added another dimension to an already heartwarming time together.

When reflecting on our special moments, the words *gathering, event, celebration, ceremony, ritual, occasion* and *happening* come to mind. What do all these words mean? People assemble for a Gathering. Something happens at an Event. A Celebration observes an Event with respect, festivity and rejoicing. A more formal act following a Ritual or Custom denotes a Ceremony. A Ritual is a formal form of conducting a Ceremony. A large important social Gathering or significant Event can be called an Occasion. An Event with a more spontaneous feel to it can be called a Happening. All these words come into play when looking into the details of Marking the Moment.

But don't worry about fine-tuning the meanings. Just sit back and enjoy the fresh look at all these Opportunities presenting themselves to you in the following pages. Your world will be expanded to include more Observances that you previously noticed. You will hear me say time and again: Trust the process and your intuition. You will be amazed and gratified about what will emerge.

Learning to Mark the Moment

In our culture, people commonly give presents to each other for special occasions. These "things" are nice, but they don't replace words, hugs, affirmations, wishes or opportunities to express appreciation for your treasured family and friends. In this first series of books about marking the significant moments in your life, you explore what is possible to enhance three distinctive stages.

Significant times in life long to be noticed. The topics and stories for each section are chosen as examples because people have already integrated this magic into their lives. They certainly don't cover all opportunities for celebration, but they do offer glimpses into what is possible. Let's look now at how the make a meaningful moment.

The Recipe

This simple four-part recipe sets you up for sweet success in marking your special moments. Thanks to a formula that is concise, clear and effective, you shift into action because you now know what to do. You'll be on your way to opening your heart to more appreciation and connection.

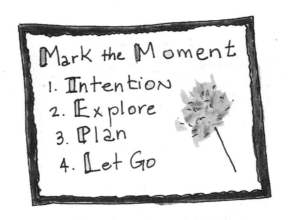

Let's look at what it takes to produce an exceptional occasion:

Set your intention: Herein lies the core of your experience. When you can pinpoint the intention, the rest of the story will follow. Intention helps move to the heart of the matter. Some intentions are easy to identify: a baby shower, a funeral, a birthday, or an anniversary. Some hide in the shadows of the unknown, as most people haven't had any experience or model to help identify them: embracing a new role (becoming a grandmother or mother-in-law), acknowledging a divorce, moving away from the neighborhood, helping a person going through chemotherapy, or struggling with a terminal illness. You will feel the nudge of unrest when a situation arises where you will ask yourself the question: "What can I do—for myself or someone else?"

Example of intention: Here is a moment from my life where I used the recipe. I was going into the hospital for hip surgery and wanted to make this experience special. How could I do this?

Explore your options. Once you've decided on your intention, you need to think about how to achieve it. Start by asking yourself many questions to release the essence of the person or occasion. For example:

- What is she doing now in her life?
- What is her living situation?
- What are her hobbies?
- What is her passion?
- Does she have a spiritual practice?
- Does she have a family?
- Who are her friends?
- Where does she work?
- Is work important to her personal well-being?
- Does she travel?
- Does she volunteer?
- What are her worries at this point in life?
- What does she need?

Brainstorm with a friend to discover more about your person or event. The more questions you ask and answer, the stronger your position to implement the plan.

Example of exploring: I asked myself many of the above questions attempting to figure out a direction to go with my intention. After some floundering, I realized that I wanted my friends to be with me in some way while I was in the hospital. I knew of a friend undergoing serious cancer treatment who had more than a hundred people show up in her hospital room. That wasn't my style, but I liked the idea of folks supporting me in some way. How could I take these friends and family with me to the hospital without actually having them there? Cards, letters, DVD's, all kinds of ideas passed through my head searching for an expression to meet my needs. I also knew I needed a new nightgown before going to the hospital and that need triggered my answer.

Make your plan: Once these questions are answered, you'll be amazed at how the plan simply unfolds. You will know where you need to be, who to invite, what to do, when to do it, because the pieces of the puzzle are in place from the exploration. If, for some reason, the plan isn't unfolding, go back to the exploration and dig deeper.

Example for the plan: Once the nightgown idea revealed itself, I was on a roll. I wanted it to be a white cotton one so that people could write on it. I happened to find the perfect nightgown in our little town. As the surgery was on Halloween Day, I found permanent markers in black, orange and purple and started carrying my nightgown around town with me. Any time I saw a friend I dragged it out and asked them to sign it. By the time of my surgery, many names graced my gown. My friends with their written good wishes would surround me. I took the nightgown with me to the hospital and hung it on the door when I needed to wear a hospital gown. Nurses commented on it. I felt love and support emanating from it. While recovering at home, I wore it night and day for three weeks.

Let go: Creating a meaningful moment takes on a life of its own once the intention is put into place and the action starts. The process will energize you as your creative juices carry you along. Once the project is launched, you need to realize that your job is done and let go of the outcome. It doesn't have to be perfect. You may find yourself wanting to rehash, judge, trying to decide if it was good enough. The recipe requires that you to put the event into the world and let it go, because it will be just what is needed, whatever happens.

Example of letting go: I had to make a conscious effort to purely enjoy my nightgown. Every once in a while, I would think of someone who I wished had signed it. I realized that even those people who had not signed the gown were thinking of me and cheering me on. I needed to look at that nightgown and wallow in the love and concern of my friends and family and remember how lucky I am. And indeed, that silly nightgown encouraged my healing.

There is no right or wrong when the intention is clear, the motivation is honorable, and love is at the core of the event.

Hopefully this example helps you glimpse the remarkable power of the recipe. Just because it's simple doesn't mean it isn't effective. You will see how it evolves in the stories and offers a structure to jump-start imagination.

Useful Tools

As you get a sense for creating a meaningful moment, you are ready to add ideas that will broaden your experience. Below are nine suggestions to encourage deep connection. Read about these tools. Get a feel for them. Then pick and choose what will work for your particular occasion. Trust your reaction when you read about each tool. Relate it to the event you are thinking about and you will know if it is appropriate for your situation. Different events will use different tools. These are the ones that have worked for me in various situations. I use what I need at that moment and save the rest for a later time.

The Circle

When I began facilitating women's health classes, I was advised to take a training course called "Peerspirit Circling," based on Christina Baldwin's book, *Calling the Circle* (Bantam, 1998). This training rocked my world in many ways, especially because we sat in a circle that was supportive, respectful and where each person was heard. I came away from this experience thinking that this is how we need to live life every day. This training laid the foundation for *Celebrating Beginnings and Endings*, as we create places where each person is held in a nurturing and positive environment.

When a group meets in a circle, all are equal and all can see each other. If there is nothing else of use from these suggestions, take the circle and put it into practice. It's easy—just a question of setting up the chairs. The unstated equality that occurs in a circle sets the stage for open communication. No person looks as if she's in charge. All are equally available. When we begin our gathering with this premise, our environment supports our intention.

The Center

The center of the circle offers a place to be creative and illustrates the intention of the gathering. In my travel bag of tools, I keep a tablecloth or something to cover the center space. With this I can transform any table, old box, bin or whatever appears, to use as the center of the circle. The cloth adds class, texture, color and helps to identify a special place. I often further define the center by adding a symbol of my purpose. If I am at a business meeting using chairs around a table, I may put the group's mission statement in the center. Adding a wedding picture of the couple sets the tone for an anniversary celebration. A pair of scissors reminds the guests of cutting the ties at a time when a divorce is being acknowledged. A fishing reel or lures may remind me of an uncle who just died. At a high school graduation party, guests who have already graduated might bring pictures of themselves at age eighteen to put on the table. This visual display at the center of the circle reminds each person of why we are there. I use my creative ideas to lead me to a visual expression to mark the uniqueness of the occasion.

The Agreements

When I meet with a group, I want to provide specific guidelines. Depending on the situation, the directives are clearly stated. At less formal occasions—what I call "sneaky circles"—I may not talk about the agreements directly, but they are still upholding me in the process. I sense when I will feel comfortable talking about the agreements or when they are too structured for less intense and less formal gatherings. The story examples will illustrate all kinds of events—some use a formal setting and some don't use any agreements. I trust my inner guidance to lead me in the appropriate direction.

Here are the four agreements that I feel are important:

 Listen carefully and respectfully

Listening carefully and respectfully means that when a person is talking, they are not to be interrupted. This puts a responsibility on each speaker to monitor her words and not to hog center stage. If someone begins to dominate a gathering, the convener needs to step in and gently remind her that others also have something to say. This can be tricky to handle, but is essential to respecting each guest. The use of a talking piece (explained later) can assist in these situations. Learning to speak and to listen are skills that come almost naturally when meeting in a defined circle.

 Leave out judgment

When judgment is left out of the circle, magic happens. Being judgmental is a pernicious habit. When I finally experienced a setting where judgment was not allowed, I noticed that people opened their hearts to a new level of honesty and acceptance. Non-judgment is truly spiritual and can change any gathering.

 Respect each other with confidentiality

It is difficult for me to have to mention confidentiality in a group setting, and sometimes I don't. I want people to realize that gossip is not a part of what we are about. Wisdom emerges from personal stories that may help others, yet the names and details need not be passed on. If a person realizes that what she says in circle stays in the circle, she is freer to express herself.

★ **Depend on a guiding Spirit (however you define that) to help hold your space**

Whenever I design an intentional gathering, I am involved with a process larger than I am. I consider myself merely a tool called to put forth an idea through which people can connect with respect and love. I know I am held up by a source greater than myself as these gatherings and events are almost sacred in that they involve the highest and best that we have to offer as humans. Most of us can't do that work alone. To indicate the presence of a higher power, I nearly always have a candle in the middle of the circle and mention that we are a part of the cosmos.

When I present any or all of these agreements, it is only fair to ask if the group will accept them as the foundation for the time together. In that way, all are choosing to participate with the same framework. If, perchance, someone needs clarification or can't accept the principles, then I may need to modify my plan and not expect to hold the deeper space that these boundaries offer.

Don't feel overwhelmed and over-structured after reading about these agreements. I am aware that they are available to use when I feel comfortable and they are personal. Many of the stories don't touch these agreements, yet they may become important when I am ready to embrace difficult issues and people may need to have a place where they can express themselves safely.

A Bell

Often when a group is meeting, people begin by standing around visiting. In order to announce the start of the gathering, a bell, whistle, gong, horn, or kazoo can alert guests to come together to begin. Use your creativity and intention to set the tone for your group. Use one of the silly sounds for a light-hearted occasion. For a more serious or intense event, use a sound that will invoke a more solemn ambiance.

My favorite starting sound comes from Tibetan finger bells called *tingshas*. They are two bronze disks held together with a lanyard. When the disks are touched together the most glorious sound penetrates the scene and suggests that something special is about to happen. That sound isn't appropriate for all occasions, so I need to stay flexible. When the group is in place, I repeat the sound to define the starting moment. When finished, I use the same sound to close the space. Defining the beginning and ending of a gathering helps focus the energy and attention of the participants. Using sound is a small detail that adds one more element to an already special occasion.

A Talking Piece

Another unique part of creating a memorable event is that each person has the opportunity to speak. We have all been in groups where one or two people dominate the conversation. Using a talking piece honors guests by giving each one the option and opportunity to speak. The talking piece is an object that is passed around the circle. When a person is holding the object, it is her turn to speak. When she is done, she passes it on to the next person. The talking piece can move in a circle or go to the next person willing to speak. When a person receives the talking piece, she is not required to speak. She can pass it on if she isn't ready to talk or doesn't have anything to say. Even though she may not want to speak, having had the chance to do so honors her presence there.

At first, this new technique may feel strange. As one becomes familiar with it the benefits of defining the speaker and giving each person an opportunity to talk, participation occurs at a new level.

The choice of talking piece offers up more opportunity to use creativity. I once used a pen when celebrating a graduation. I use a tampon when starting a menopause class. A little ball can be tossed around for a lighthearted object. The sketch shows a talking piece that was made by a dear friend of mine. Use your imagination to connect to your intention. The talking piece offers yet another ingredient to a gathering that ties all the elements together to add continuity, imagination and even fun, to any occasion.

A Small Kitchen Timer

At more formal meetings where people may be discussing issues in pairs or small groups, I sometimes choose to set a specific time period. When the timer goes off, it's time to move on. A kitchen timer helps set boundaries in a non-threatening way. For example, the timer works well when I have a large group—more than twelve people—who are all eager to  talk. I may break them into four groups of three people and ask a specific question— what do you need to finish this project? I set the timer for three minutes and one person is allowed to speak without in- terruption for that amount of time. When the timer goes off, the next person speaks, then the third. In this way, each per- son has a chance to speak and be heard without taking up the time in a large group. No feedback is necessary or even invited. To finish the process, I may ask for a quick synopsis from each group. Make your own variations to work for your setting

The timer can save me when I have a person who is so eager to talk that she can't stop herself. Instead of having to cut her off, I can implement the use of the timer and that solves the problem.

Invitations

Sending invitations helps express intention. When I am clear with others about my plan, the guests can be mentally prepared to participate. The purpose may be as simple as stating that I am giving a tea where friends will have an opportunity to tell my mom that they appreciate her. A more complicated issue could include addressing an intense question—"What supported you when things got tough in your marriage?"—for a wedding shower. I may ask people to bring specific gifts like poems, flowers, or a symbolic representation to support the intention of the gathering. At a recent party, the birthday woman asked each guest to bring a rock. The variety of rocks and the stories that went with them kept everyone laughing, even crying, and amazed at the power of a simple rock.

The flavor of the invitation sets the tone of the gathering even before the guests arrive. If I use snail mail for delivery, particular colors invoke certain feelings. The type of font signifies a formal or informal quality. Choice of graphics can uphold the intention. Instructions alert the guests to be prepared. Invitations can also be made by phone calls or electronically. I try to be aware that whatever I choose is deliberate and supports my overall offering.

If you have given a party recently and wanted to know who was coming, you may have noticed that few people these days honor the old tradition of RSVP, which comes from the French phrase *respondez s'il vous plaît*, which translates to "please respond." It doesn't mean to answer if you feel like it, or answer only if you are coming. Perhaps the tradition is lost to the upcoming generation. The bottom line question for the person giving the party is how to find out how many guests will arrive.

In order to achieve your goal of hearing from your friends, you may have to resort to a newer creative plan. I have received Evites (an on-line invitation site) where everyone has access the list of guests, who is coming, who is not and who hasn't yet responded. Perhaps the openness of the invitation will encourage people to reply.

Email itself is a great tool. If you send snail mail invitations yet also have emails of your guests, you can then gently prod them with an email reminder.

You also may want to reword the RSVP so that it is more direct and your guests will truly understand that you want a reply. In your invitation you might want to try something like:

- I need to know who is coming. Please email or call
- If I don't hear from you by _____, I will assume you can't come.

◆ Work with the theme of the gathering to choose what kind of response is appropriate. A more formal affair may merit an old fashioned RSVP, but for a beer bash, you can be more direct and funny—I need to know if you are coming so I know how many kegs to order.

◆ Alternative and creative measures will work. You can come up with a suitable idea to solve the problem. Have fun with it.

Tool Kit

I have developed a tool kit for myself that I find handy. Mine is in a lovely handmade bag that I can grab whenever I think I may need it. Included are:

1. Tingshas (or a bell) to bring people together, begin and end a gathering
2. A small candle and a match (important to have the match handy as well)
3. An assortment of talking pieces
4. A timer
5. A cloth to use for a centering space

My basic tools are ready at a moment's notice. I can grab it and run when I think I may require of any of these delightful tools. All I need to add is something appropriate for the center space. For me, this purse is my doctor kit for the soul.

Silence

Silence is underrated. If a group is silent, it may seem as if something is wrong. Commonly, someone will break the quiet just to fill the void, even though she may not have anything particularly pertinent to say. When I am part of an intentional gathering, I may want to remind my group of the power of silence. When people are given moments of unstructured, quiet time, special insights may present themselves. When space is constantly being filled verbally, one may miss a significant moment of processing or understanding. Remember that old saying "Silence is golden."

From these nine tools I pick and choose what will work after establishing my intention. Once the pieces are in place, I relax and let the spontaneous part of the event unfold. When the details are carefully presented, then the magic of the moment will take over and whisk everyone to a new world of connection with friends, loved ones, and business associates.

Now that you have the tools handy, use your intuition to create what you want and crave, where hearts are connected, people communicate, and the possibility of healing can take place.

I am choosing to use the female pronoun throughout the book, as traditionally mothers and grandmothers create ritual for the family. They are generally the keepers of history and caretakers of the stories. My guess is that it will predominantly be women who will want to produce these new practices. I hope that men will also work to claim their place to become guides for creating traditions and circles.

You will notice that it seldom takes lots of money to create the experience. Because you depend on your ingenuity and creative juices, the plan flows without a huge financial outlay, which leaves the door open for anyone brave enough to step through the portal.

Nearly all the stories come from personal experience—either mine or someone else's. Names have been changed, except for my close family. I am grateful to the many people who have shared their ideas, so the rest of us can be inspired.

I invite you to read this book with pencil in hand. There is plenty of room in the margins to jot down ideas as you are reading. Seize the moment when you have an inspiration. Don't lose that brilliant thought. These vivid *ah-ha!* moments can escape like a dream if you don't nail them down at the moment when they decide to materialize. Use this as your journal so you can refer to it when opportunity is knocking.

You will develop the tools to create meaningful moments when life may not be easy or happy. Meaningful moments come in all kinds of packages. They include grief as well as joy, discomfort as well as harmony, and hurt as well as healing. The intention gives direction on how to fully experience opportunities in our lives. Be ready for an awakening of the heart as you create what you desire.

This process of collecting the stories has provided me with unexpected delight. Each interview showed me what a person has done to create a meaningful moment. From acknowledging a miscarriage, to being on the receiving end of a huge appreciation, these stories will grab you and encourage you to want to have some of this joy (and even healing) in your life. I thank each of you who contributed to this work of love, which is meant to model a new way of coming together. We can all be initiators for our circle of friends and family. Take the lead and move forward.

Getting Started

When I purchase a "how to" book, I want to know exactly what to do to begin. Here are five ideas to use immediately. After you've read the back cover of this book, checked out my photo, skimmed through the introduction, and read the recipe, let's get started!

 Look for opportunity

You may already have an occasion in mind for your first meaningful moment. If so, you're good to go. If not, then begin to be aware of opportunities in your life where you can be proactive and offer a original sort of event. Maybe your sister had a miscarriage. Maybe your daughter is thirteen and coming of age. Maybe your dad has just been diagnosed with terminal cancer. Maybe a friend recently went through a painful divorce. You yourself are going through menopause. These examples may help to open your eyes to the scenes around you that can be highlighted.

 Start with appreciation

Everyone wants to feel appreciated. You can't go wrong by choosing a worthy person to practice on. An ordinary visit by a special person turns into a memorable stay if you take the time to tell them what they mean to you. A man in your office is changing jobs. Don't let him leave without taking a few minutes to let him know that he made a difference by being there. Your neighbors are moving. Let them know that you were glad to share the neighborhood with them for so many years. Small life changes happen every day. We can choose to mark them with gratitude and appreciation. Each of us can play a part in adding this dimension of positive energy to everyday occurrences.

 Try a practice run

Pick a happy event, such as an appreciation circle. Use this occasion to practice some of the ideas and tools offered. For example, your mom is coming for a visit. You invite several of her friends to tea in her honor. Tell her friends that there will be a time to tell her how they appreciate her and what she means to them. You have tea together, then move into the living room and sit in a circle around a small, delicately decorated table with flowers, a candle, and a picture of your mom on it. To start the sharing time, you can ask guests to tell how they met your mom, and then say what they admire or appreciate about her.

This isn't about packages. This is about taking the time to share what we know and love about people in our lives. The event isn't expensive or complicated, but the benefits of connection and having an opportunity to express to people that we care is precious. This small ritual packs a powerful punch, yet is easy, inexpensive and straightforward to produce. As a practice run, choose something accessible to begin. You will be so pleased with the results you will be encouraged to try again soon—perhaps in a more complex situation.

 Start simply.

Our example is simple—not too many people, uncomplicated food, no presents, supportive friends willing to help you on your first attempt with a new experiment, doing it at home, avoiding fancy decoration, a short time period, and focusing on the intention of honoring your mom. As you plan your first event, notice what you can leave out what doesn't support your purpose. By keeping your eye on the goal, you can offer an easy, yet effective, gathering to help build your confidence.

 Enlist a friend to help you

The right partner generates fun, zest and energy for your project. Rather than planning all alone, especially when you are trying out a new idea, a friend can help stretch your imagination and push your comfort level. Brainstorming infuses new life and vigor into what can seem like a lonely road. Either co-chair the event or ask for advice for the planning part. You will be sharing the message of how to create meaningful moments with another person who may also see the value and implement an event for herself.

33

You are now ready to make your own positive contribution. You have five ideas to start a simple practice run. Be brave and take the first leap!

If you feel comfortable with the concepts, move into the body of the book. Nearly one hundred stories are available to inspire you. The recipe, ideas for getting started, and tools will help you design your first project. Be prepared for a delightful change in your life. You will transform ordinary occasions into meaningful moments. You become a creator of defining valued events. Be courageous and begin the journey.

Part I: Beginnings

With our recipe, tools and encouragement in place, begin to read the stories of what people have done in their lives to honor special times. Beginnings exist in many settings. It's up to you to notice them, decide to act and mark your moment. As you read these stories, be prepared to be delighted at people's creativity and uniqueness, realizing that this, too, can become your reality. Enjoy the uplifting feeling when you read these demonstrations of courage and love.

Birth: Welcoming a Child into the World

What is more appropriate than birth for our beginning? A new child in the world offers a rich opportunity to honor the baby, the parents, the space where they will live, the already-existing siblings, the grandparents and extended family and friends. The actual birth process itself—as well as preparation for it—already creates special moments. As we grow to understand our role in adding more meaning to our lives, this birth time is opportunity knocking with a loud beat.

Our first story is a bit unusual, as it talks about preparing the place where the baby will live. The new mom and I designed the event, and this is what we did:

Blessing the Birth Space

Ben and Sally's first baby was due near the holidays. I wanted to do something for them, but not necessarily a traditional shower. The birth time was getting close and I needed to move into action if anything was going to be done. I called Sally, saying that I wanted to offer to plan something. What would she like? Very quickly she said she was dreaming of a time with close friends to prepare the living space for the baby—not in the physical sense of painting and remodeling, but of welcoming the child into the world even before she arrived. I was thrilled with this idea and excited to be part of making it happen.

Sally and I started putting it together. Sally was very clear about who she and Ben wanted to attend—those folks who would understand and support the idea of a pre-birth housewarming. I called the guests on the phone, as it was short notice. The parents wanted the gathering to take place in the location where the baby would be living.

The intention was to prepare a community nest for the baby. The nest would be made of stories, poetry, wisdom, favorite children's books, lullabies or handmade items. The offering for the event would come from the heart of each guest. We trusted that each person knew what this new being needed to smooth the transition into the world, help her be comfortable and accepted before her actual arrival.

When the evening arrived, we gathered—men and women— in a circle in the living room of the home where the child would be living. A candle was lit in honor of the baby. We passed around a rattle to use as a talking piece. A friend acted as host/facilitator. The offerings included live music presentations, the start of the child's own library, special Christmas ornaments, wisdom for parenting, and stories from childhood. Best of all was the overwhelming sense of how wanted and special this child was— even before she entered the world. Blessings on this loving home and caring parents were offered. Afterwards we ate, drank and laughed.

The actual birth time a few days later turned out to be very difficult for Sally. One of the things that helped her stay focused was remembering the support of those who had assisted in preparing the home for the child.

Because Sally had a clear vision, I was able to help make it happen. In this case, I was less a creator and more an enabler. I didn't need to agonize on what to do, as Sally knew what she wanted and I could act as the helper. Sally designed her own evening.

The next story tells of a spontaneous way to mark the birth of a second child. Be prepared to smile when you hear what happened.

Special Welcome for a Second Child

Christy and Rick were expecting their second child. Christy originally planned a traditional hospital birth. When Rick suggested using a midwife, Christy immediately said, "No way!" However, after pondering the idea, she went to the library to do research on midwifery. She found that she liked what she discovered and decided to keep the door open for an alternative to hospital delivery. In their vicinity, there was an excellent midwife practitioner. Ultimately, Christy and Rick both felt confident that using a midwife was the correct decision for them.

In looking at an impending childbirth celebration, each parent needs to establish his or her intent for this occasion in order to create something out of the ordinary. For Christy and Rick, their goals were to be safe and surrounded by those who would assist them and uphold them in love. They both felt that childbirth is a natural process, as opposed to a medical condition. Taking the usual precautions with good prenatal care, it looked like their delivery would be normal. They were granted the opportunity to use the services of the midwife and make a comfortable atmosphere where they were able to create the space of their dreams.

Christy told me of a beautiful time with her older daughter, Anne, and the new baby *in utero*. Anne would rub her mommy's tummy. She would talk to the new baby and sing songs to her. She was welcoming their new baby before it arrived. From what we know about babies *in utero*, this pre-birth bonding and acceptance will be significant in the development of this child in the years to come. Christy was sensitive to notice the opportunity, which presented itself to the three of them, and allow it to develop. Christy unexpectedly created a meaningful moment by being aware of the bonding time and flowed with it.

From the time Christy went into labor, she, Rick and Anne were surrounded with the people who were important to them in a loving and supportive way. The midwife was a knowledgeable delivery person. She had an apprentice assisting her. A *doula* (a person who provides non-medical and non-midwifery support) acted as the emotional advocate for the mom. Rick supported Christy. Little Anne was there with a guardian to take care of her. The lights were low. Candles and soft music filled the room, giving it a dreamy quality. The baby arrived in a water bath, moving from amniotic fluid to a warm tub. The family honored the connecting time that this birth offered. This finely tuned team worked together to receive the baby into the world in the least stressful way possible and supported Christy. They created several extraordinary experiences for themselves during the prenatal and birthing time.

Countless women asked me if I was including the Blessing Way in this book. I decided I had better heed the message.

Blessing Way

The Blessing Way is a ceremony reestablishing a Native American tradition of honoring transitions. In this case, acknowledging the move into motherhood. The midwife or whoever is offering the gathering designs an intentional space. A Blessing Way is done in place of a traditional shower, as the mother is being showered not by things and games, but by wisdom, stories, love and support.

If this touches your heart and you want to know more, please use the Internet to gather further information. I am here to plant the seed for you.

The following story is a lovely example of how one woman used the age-old tradition to honor her baby.

Mimi's Blessing Way

Mimi's second baby was due April 17, and she wanted to mark the event with something more meaningful than a baby shower. Those can by fun, but she wanted a way to deeply honor and celebrate not only the coming of this baby, but her own passage into motherhood again. Thankfully, she had a wonderfully supportive community of women friends, and two of them offered to host a blessing way ceremony. This Navajo tradition can be used to acknowledge any life transition.

Twelve of her closest friends attended this special get-together. The hostess created a beautiful alter with fresh flowers, lavender candles, a photo of Mimi's son, and photos of other women's children. The afternoon began by reading a poem about birth, and then each woman introduced herself by maternal lineage ("I am Mimi, daughter of Amanda, granddaughter of Betty and Alice"). Then a bowl was passed around into which each woman placed a bead she had chosen, to eventually be made into a necklace that Mimi planned to have with her during her birthing time. With her bead, each woman offered a poem, story, or blessing for either the new mom, or the baby, or both of them. After drying their tears from that moving ritual, they were surprised by an unexpected guest . . . a local musician who led them in an hour of songs and chants to celebrate birth and womanhood. The singing was fun and strengthened the bonding. After the music, they had a wonderful lunch of fresh food made by a few of the guests and the hosts. The last part of the ceremony included indulging Mimi. She relaxed in a comfy chair while the women took turns painting her big beautiful belly with henna designs, washing and massaging her feet, and bringing her chocolate and strawberries to eat! The whole day was truly splendid and more perfect than she imagined. Mimi gave each woman a candle to light for her when her birthing time began. The necklace would be a wonderful reminder of the love and positive energy that she would take with her as she delivered her baby girl into the world.

The next story demonstrates a more formal and planned celebration, variations on a shower theme, but carrying the evening to a new depth and connection.

Feathering the Nest

I want to offer to you an outline of a shower we gave for a young couple. It is unusual, in my experience, to have such an ordered plan. In this case, it was just what we needed, and gave us form from which to flow. Several people were planning different parts of this presentation. I will also include the invitation. This example is a very practical application of marking a moment.

Jasmine and Dan's New Baby

Date: Saturday, January 23 Time: 7:30 Place: *******, *****, ***

Please come to Feather the Nest with Love and Blessings to Welcome Jasmine and Dan's Baby

Bring: Stories, music, poems, and tokens. You can share how you hon-or your special relationship with this child (as uncle, parent, friend, grandparent), or how you dream and vision your life with this new being. Be open to what comes to you.

Refreshments will be offered

RSVP: Paula @***-**** or Dana @ ***-****
Directions: ***

Here are the steps we took:

- **Have lullaby music playing while people arrive**

- **WHY are we here? The intent of this group is:**

   We are calling a circle to honor the coming of the baby—to bless this house where the baby will live by our presence here

- **HOW are we going to do this?**

   There will be an opportunity for each of you to speak if you feel so inclined—to share from your heart what happens when you think about this baby—what's your vision of her place in your life and heart? Do you have some wisdom to share from your experience with children? Is there something significant from your experience as a child that would uphold Jasmine and Dan in their parenting role? The possibilities are unlimited. There are no grades on this—this is a time and place where judgment is suspended, where there is no right or wrong. What comes from your heart just *is*.

- **Kathy: talks about awkwardness**

   Kathy explains that this format might be different for some of the guests. Please relax into the flow and trust the process. Each person will be given the opportunity to speak and they can pass if they have nothing to say or are shy.

- **Centering Table: introduce it and what is on it**

    Pat does the explanation of the table

- **Candle**

    Kathy informs the group that the candle symbolizes the spirit of the child who is already with us. We are acknowledging this new being joining us spiritually as well as within Jasmine physically. Light the candle.

- **Rattle**

    Dot explains that the rattle will be passed around and used as a talking piece. We chose this practical symbol (practical in that it will stay with Jasmine and Dan) as it is representative of the warrior archetype as brought forth in *The Four-Fold Way* by Angeles Arrien (1993, HarperCollins). Why is this important? Ms. Arrien compiles myth, archetypes and stories from indigenous cultures throughout the world and throughout history. She helps to connect us to our heritage and the rich resources brought to us from other cultures and time periods. The Rattle is the symbol of the Winter season, which is the time of year this baby comes to us in physical form. The archetype of this season is the warrior (there are four archetypes— warrior, healer, teacher and visionary—all of us have a bit of each of them in us). We are honoring the warrior in this baby on this day. For clarification, an archetype is the original pattern or model from which all things of the same type are made—a prototype, so to speak. The warrior in each of us has surfaced because we have shown up—Showing Up is one of the guiding principles of the warrior archetype.

Nest

Each season has its special animal and for Winter it is the winged creature. We chose a bird's nest as symbolic of this house being the nest of the baby. We are symbolically feathering the Nest with our stories, our presence, dreams and visions. As the Rattle comes around and if you don't feel the need to speak, please take a feather from the basket and put it in the bird's nest—being here is a powerful witness in itself.

How To

We will do two rounds with the rattle. One will be a practice one where we will give our names and relationship to the baby and its family. The next round will be for each of you to feather the nest in your own special way—with the physical feather and your verbal contribution. When we finish that one, we will return for one more round just in case you are inspired to add something else. We need to listen attentively without judgment. Whoever has the Rattle has our attention without interruption. Are there any questions? Let us begin.

So the evening unfolds. . . .

■ **Closure**

Sit for a moment focusing our love and attention on the Candle, on the Baby, and the experience of being together as a community and family to welcome this child into the world.

■ **Finally**

Does anyone have a special nursery song to sing?
When done, blow out the Candle, give a final shake of the Rattle and eat!

This last account doesn't tell a story per se, but gives you a fairly concrete example of a project that was rather formal and planned. You can visualize what this group has done to make the presentation flow smoothly. Many meaningful moments are less structured and more spontaneous, even though the intention is clear. You will know what is right for your occasion.

Here is a lovely shower where the focus is on the new mom more than the up-coming baby. Friends were delighted to support their friend as she moved into her new parenting role.

A Shower of Affirmation

Our daughter, Melissa, was pregnant with our first grandchild. Her friend, Tianna, my daughter, Katie, and I planned to host a baby shower for her local friends to be held in Melissa's home. The location is significant as I live five hours' drive away, and Tianna lives two hours away.

A Baby Shower!!

The three of us principals emailed and telephone consulted until we had a plan.

- Women only
- Time and a date
- A Brunch
- A joint gift of a stroller
- A surprise activity

The bare bones were in place.

Melissa compiled the guest list with addresses. Katie offered to make the invitations. I addressed and mailed them. Tianna and I arrived a day early in the afternoon in time to buy our food supplies. The day of the shower we made the quiches, muffins and fruit salad. Melissa's grandmother had already made a frozen raspberry dessert. We were ready.

On the appointed day, the twelve guests arrived and we ate our delicious brunch. We then gathered in a circle where each woman introduced herself and how she knew Melissa. Wonderful stories emerged as each person explained the relationship between the two women. The power of hearing each guest speak created an immediate connection and set a space where each person was honored.

The invitation said: "There will be a picture frame with a large mat. The frame will hold a picture of Melissa and the baby when one is available, and we will write on the mat! So, get ready to finish the sentence: "I hope you have your mother's_____."

As we went around the circle again, each woman offered a word or a phrase along with an explanation of why she chose it, and then wrote it on the mat. These affirmations surrounded the empty place where picture would go. Later on, when Melissa felt overwhelmed with mothering, she could reread these words and perhaps be prepared to make it through another day.

"I hope you have your mother's":

- Musical soul
- Integrity and empathy
- Energy, smarts and musical ability
- Beauty inside and out
- Joyful heart and quick mind
- Zeal
- Sense of adventure
- Personality, friendliness, and ability to make everyone feel comfortable and welcome
- A sense of humor and a sense of wonder
- Loyalty
- Strength and power balanced with endless compassion

Afterwards, we examined the details of the handsome stroller that was purchased by the group.

This celebration honored each woman present including the mother-to-be. The picture frame acted as a reminder for Melissa to remember herself as a competent woman, as well as her new role of mother. It acted as a mirror from her friends, giving her value and support for this new task.

At the end of the day, the group felt bonded as we learned more about Melissa. The entire project turned out to be a delight. Chores were shared. The format was simple, yet heartfelt and well thought-out. Everyone was pleased with the unusual "shower" of verbal gifts and affirmations. The circle of local women was ready to receive this new baby.

Graduations: Celebrating Accomplishment

Graduations from many kinds of institutions and programs offer us an opportunity to single out the individual for special attention. Accomplishment at some level has been reached. What a great time to seize the moment and create an occasion to honor this person. The work of the program is done (an ending) opening the way for what's next (a beginning). The various levels of accomplishment may dictate the appropriate response. Graduation from kindergarten won't normally warrant the same festivity as a college graduation, yet depending on the circumstances, finishing that first year at school might be a major success story.

The first story illustrates how a family tuned into a graduate, observing her interests, and even thinking ahead to a future project. We see how the process works and is fun and effective.

A Graduation Quilt

Recently I was talking about creating meaningful moments with my nieces, Sonja and Britt, while visiting my mom. The girls seemed interested and asked lots of questions. After they left, I realized that Sonja was about to graduate from college and my reputation as the "meaningful moment" lady was going to be on the line. Opportunity was knocking, and I was determined to produce.

My intention was clear: to celebrate Sonja's college graduation. It was especially important to me to validate and honor Sonja at this time since her mother had recently passed away.

As I moved into the exploration phase of the recipe, I enlisted the help of my mom to brainstorm with me about Sonja's life. We tried to put ourselves in her shoes. What is she doing? What are her passions? What are her plans? Is she going to travel? Is she going to look for a new job? Is she going to graduate school?

Mom reminded me that she had already given Sonja a sewing machine as her college graduation gift. Sonja had never learned to sew, as she was too busy taking classes and playing volleyball. As Mom and I tossed around ideas, we realized that we could use the sewing machine as the basis for the celebration. We decided to ask family members and friends to each send Sonja a yard of fabric with an explanation of why they picked that particular pattern. The fabric would become the material she needed to make a quilt that reflected the patchwork of her life. We chose a color theme of blue to tie the fabrics together.

The word got around quickly. Family members who couldn't attend the graduation ceremony were excited to be included. They had fun picking out fabric for Sonja that connected with her interests. The project took on a life of its own.

When Sonja started opening the packages at her party, she was puzzled at first to be receiving a yard of fabric with a story, but was delighted when she finally caught on. Twenty-five people sent fabrics and stories. A cousin gave a pattern with anchors on it, as this is the symbol of her sorority. Her dad found material that featured the state of Colorado as a reminder of where Sonja went to college. There were flowers to symbolize her love of gardening; music to remind her of playing the violin; sport motifs because she was a volleyball player. These were all meant to be a part of her memory quilt. The project was fun, practical, and created a meaningful moment as Sonja's life unfolded with the stories.

I did need to remind myself of the letting go part of the formula. If some of the colors didn't match, so what? If all the packages weren't wrapped, who cared? If Sonja never got around to making the quilt, it wasn't for me to be upset about it. My job was to offer the project and let it unfold.

This unusual plan that revealed itself to us was inexpensive, included people who couldn't attend, was creative, and gave Sonja a sense of being valued at the same time as celebrating her academic accomplishment.

The next story is a bit unusual as this person hadn't yet graduated, but her family and friends felt that she needed a lift to make it to the final diploma. Notice what these creative people arranged to support this young woman on her passage to completion.

Finishing Half of Medical School

Leah is going to medical school, which is very challenging for her. She keeps asking herself hard questions. Will she be a good doctor when she finally finishes? Is she in the right profession? Does she have the tenacity to finish the course?

One day, her family realized that Leah had passed the halfway mark. The main basic sciences were done. She was finally moving into her clinic-based work. The picture of being a doctor was beginning to emerge. Leah's mom, Carol, decided it was time to acknowledge Leah's accomplishment—to celebrate the halfway point. At this moment, Leah was a bit in the dumps about the commitment. She was forgetting about how much that she had already accomplished. She was tired.

Thinking about the intention, Carol decided that a party where Leah was surrounded by her friends and family could boost her spirits. A space where people could tell Leah about why they thought she would be a good doctor might encourage her. By seeing herself through others' eyes, she might realize that she could move ahead with her dream. Carol knew that Leah would be apprehensive if she thought there would be a celebration for her, so the party had to be a surprise. Carol didn't live where Leah was going to school, and didn't know whom to invite. She was able to obtain the phone number of one of Leah's close friends. Carol called Janice to feel her out on the idea of having a party for Leah and to ask if she would help. Janice was immediately excited about the project and offered to contact Leah's friends and invite them to the celebration

The celebration took some planning, as the hostesses were not in the same town. When Leah's friends found out about the idea, they were all eager to lend a hand and so the logistics were not difficult. Carol got the food and supplies. Janice gathered the guests.

Leah's family took her out to dinner on the evening of the party. When they were away from her house, the guests slipped silently into the house to await Leah's return. She was totally unprepared for a surprise party, and gasped in delight when she realized what was happening. The only gifts were verbal. They feasted on a symbolic half cake and champagne.

After the cake and champagne, the guests sat in a circle, introduced themselves, and explained how they had met Leah. For Carol and the rest of the family, this was a wonderful way to meet Leah's friends, as well as a comfortable way to move into a space of listening more intently to each other. Then each person spoke to Leah about what they thought she would bring to the medical profession.

When the evening was over, Leah appeared to be on Cloud Nine. Very seldom had people taken the time to express affirmations about her in her presence. Leah's self-esteem and confidence had a boost that might keep her going through the next two and a half years. She could begin to see a bigger picture outside the daily grind of classes and school. She could feel that her caring and compassion were appreciated, and that being a doctor was more than an academic accomplishment. Leah told Carol that it was the best day of her life. Leah's grandparents knew about the party, and they too participated by sending cards to be read.

Many of Leah's friends were also students and began to see themselves in a larger picture, envisioning all of them moving into the world to assist those in need, and helping themselves on their personal journeys toward wellness and balance.

Graduations: Celebrating Accomplishment

Our next story is an example of seizing the moment. Our ceremony wasn't planned ahead, yet evolved in a very natural way for this college graduate. Be on the lookout for times when you might be able to insert a little heart into a gathering. You may be surprised how often this can happen and how the experience enriches the lives of all who are present.

Graduation Rose

Some years ago, my niece, Britt, was graduating from college. This was before I realized I would be writing this book. It was Britt who reminded me of this story as I was starting the manuscript.

More than twenty family and friends gathered to witness Britt's graduation. It was a lovely day with the lilacs blooming fully, as only happens in the Midwest. Most of us were from out of town and staying in a nice motel, which had an inviting, enclosed courtyard with chairs and tables. After the ceremony, we gathered informally in the courtyard, and it seemed as if something more was needed to conclude this auspicious occasion. I picked out a rose from one of the beautiful bouquets on the table, requested attention, and gathered the family into a closer circle. I asked for people who wanted to respond to the question: "What do you admire most about Britt?" As I recall, everyone present chose to speak to the question. Britt had a chance to hear wonderful affirmations about herself. Her boyfriend mentioned how he would never have considered college if it wasn't for Britt's encouragement, as no one in his family had been to college. One aunt admired her determination, as learning didn't come easily to this wonderful girl. The underlying feeling was that we all were glad to have a place and time where we could speak to Britt about how we felt about her and her accomplishment. Sometimes people do this with cards, and that is a lovely avenue for communication. To be able to express a sentiment aloud, and have the thoughts witnessed by your family/friend group is an even more powerful statement.

This gathering turned out to be a lot of fun, and at the same time, it allowed for some touching memories about the trials of growing up.

High School Pictures

Cousins Maggie and Aaron were both graduating from high school. They lived in different states but were meeting at a mini-family reunion a couple of weeks prior to the real graduations. The family wanted to celebrate the occasions while they were altogether.

Several weeks before the gathering, their Aunt Penny sent out an email to those coming asking them to bring a copy of their high school graduation photo. She also asked the family to think about the question "What was it like when you first left home?" The group met in the living room with chairs and sofas arranged in a circle. They placed the photos on a centering table early on, so the giggles would be done before they started.

Seeing the pictures of aunts, uncles and grandparents at age eighteen reminded the graduates that their family members had once been young. Lots of laughing and reminiscing resulted from seeing the photos. Penny bought two large pillar candles and decorated them with colored raffia and feathers. The feathers signified that the kids were leaving the nest—flying away to their new lives.

To begin, she introduced what they were going to do, and each of the graduates lit their own candle. A pen was used as a talking piece as it symbolized their academic world. As the pen was passed, each person answered the question about leaving home. This is a close family, yet the richness of each person's experiences was funny, deep, insightful, and sometimes courageous. They learned about each other in a new way. The graduates were riveted to the stories, as their time to leave home was close at hand. There were three high school-age nieces also present. After the adults had spoken, Penny offered the pen to the younger girls to see if they had a response to what they had just heard. Each of them made a few appropriate remarks. Then the graduates were invited to speak. A last invita-

63

tion to the group was made for any additional comments. One aunt taped the evening for her husband who couldn't come, and was planning to make duplicate tapes for each of the graduates.

In this instance, everyone chose to participate verbally. Each person knew that she had a right to pass if she didn't have anything to say, was scared, or just needed to support the graduates by her presence. Each story was accepted. There was no competition as to who had the best story, or the funniest, or the saddest. Each story was the experience and perception of the person telling it. When they were done, Penny felt as though the adults had been on a journey of reconnecting to their younger selves, and of connecting to the graduates, by taking the time to share a significant time of their lives. As the younger girls spoke, they were also feeling a part of the group as the history of their family was being opened before their eyes.

This simple, yet profound, celebration, served to:

- Honor the graduates
- Connect the adults with who they were when they were at eighteen
- Share stories about personal life journeys
- Gather the younger children into the family history loop
- Create a new family story

The gathering was inexpensive. A little planning to bring the photos and think about the question was all that was required. All felt uplifted by hearing the stories of family members, as well as honoring the graduates with gifts from the heart. The graduates took their candles with them so they had a tangible reminder of the day.

This young man worked hard to overcome a reading disability. His informal graduation underscores his achievement and honors his tenacity as he moves on in his life that has been forever changed.

Karl Can Read

Karl was an adorable six-year-old attending public school. His mom, Tina, supported him in the classroom by working there one day a week. His dad spent weekends with him doing father/son projects around the house. His older sister loved to play with him building a tree fort and inventing spy games. He was basically a happy and well-adjusted kid. As Karl proceeded from first to second grade, he started having trouble at school with his reading. Spelling and phonics were tough for him. Tina started to notice that his attitude toward school was not as good as it had been. His classroom behavior was deteriorating. What was happening to her special boy? Tina realized that something needed to be done, and soon. She worked with the classroom teacher who suggested that he have his eyes tested. His eyes were fine, and Tina was steered to a specialist in child development who knew about how the mind processes information. Karl underwent a huge battery of tests to evaluate his situation, and it was diagnosed that

Karl's mind processed information in a different way from the system that the public school was using. He was bright and he could learn, but he needed an alternate approach to learning to read. The expert recommended a program of one-on-one tutoring for Karl for several months.

Karl knew that things weren't going well in the classroom and that he was getting behind. He agreed to work with the tutor five days a week for three months in addition to his regular public school class.

Halfway through the three-month commitment, the tutors, Karl and Tina evaluated Karl's progress and agreed that the program seemed to be working. Karl was taking his work very seriously and could see for himself that he was improving.

As Tina watched Karl work so hard, she felt the family needed to acknowledge his accomplishment when he finished. What could they do that would recognize his achievement? After thinking about it, they decided to have a reading party and invite Karl's grandparents, teacher and several family members who knew about his struggle. The party 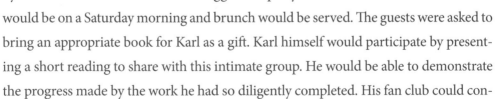 would be on a Saturday morning and brunch would be served. The guests were asked to bring an appropriate book for Karl as a gift. Karl himself would participate by presenting a short reading to share with this intimate group. He would be able to demonstrate the progress made by the work he had so diligently completed. His fan club could congratulate him for finishing his course and reaching his goal of learning to read.

When you read this heartwarming story, you will truly understand the importance of taking the time to connect and honor your loved ones. As this young man is leaving home, he departs with the gifts of love, support and blessing because his mom created a place for this to happen.

Advice and Encouragement

When her son graduated from high school a couple of years ago, Amy gave a great deal of thought about how to create an event that would help him mark this time as an important passage, and how to weave a meaningful experience for diverse parts of her family and friendship group. All four of Brad's grandparents were coming, as was his father, Amy's new partner, his younger sister, an aunt and uncle, and some friends. It was the first time these people had gathered together.

Brad is a thoughtful young man, who genuinely enjoys the company of both adults and peers. Together, he and Amy created a plan to have a potluck supper at their house after the graduation ceremony, to be followed by a circle where people could offer him good wishes and advice for the future. They sent out an invitation describing their intention for the gathering.

After a long and too-hot graduation ceremony, the group traveled to their home to share good food and conversation. When the food was finished and dishes were done, Amy invited people into the living room. "Thank you for coming to share this event in our lives. As we said in the invitation, we want to gather in circle to give each of you an opportunity to say something to Brad to help mark this transition time in his life—congratulations, advice, whatever you wish. The circle will begin with whoever wishes to speak first and moves on from there. If you're not ready to speak, simply pass and we'll come back around."

Everyone was silent looking at the collection of presents, Brad's graduation picture, and the candle burning on an end table in the center of the circle. "I'll speak first," said his paternal grandmother. "When I found out our first grandchild was going to be adopted from Korea, I didn't know how I'd feel about having a grandchild so different from myself. But from the day I met Brad, he has been our grandchild in every way. We are so proud of him."

Next his paternal grandfather spoke a similar accolade. His fifteen-year-old-sister passed. Her friend thanked Brad for being a good friend to her and wished him well. One by one, they offered advice and appreciation to this young man. Amy said she didn't actually remember what she or her partner said. She does remember that Brad's father read a thoughtful essay on the difference between achievement and success. When the circle came back around to Brad's sister, Samantha, she was silent for a moment then burst into tears. "I am going to miss you so much!" No one said anything while Samantha sobbed. Then Brad spoke. He repeated much of what had been said to him, thanking the guests for the kindness and wisdom, and spoke of his own dreams. He was speaking to them as a man, not as an eighteen-year-old who hadn't yet left home. It was as if the collective wisdom and energy in the room had gathered in him and coalesced into what everyone was feeling. And when he had finished, Brad said, "Samantha, come sit on my lap and help me open these presents." The circle moved into an easy conversational mode of people chatting about the gifts that had been brought. Afterwards in the kitchen, when Amy and her mother were cleaning up the dessert dishes, she said, "Amy, that was the most amazing gathering. Most people don't get to hear that kind of praise and support in their entire lifetime."

Traditional Religious Beginnings:
Joining the Faith Family

Many mainstream churches and synagogues in the U.S. have rituals/sacraments to mark passages that begin a new role for a child or young adult. I want us to look at how we can reflect on these occasions and add our personal touch to an already significant time.

For example, in order to write about baptism I needed to research more about the meaning of it. As I read, I realized that each faith tradition has a slightly different slant on what it means. It is important for each family to fully understand why they are participating in this ceremony and what it means to their family and particular church. When you delve into this, probably with the help of your pastor, minister, rabbi, or priest, you will grow to understand what is important to you and your spiritual circle. As you explore the meaning and intention, follow the recipe and create your own celebration, you infuse the occasion with special spiritual energy and understanding.

Be aware of why we mark any occasion. Dig into the meaning, the historical significance, the commercial exploitation, the spiritual sense, what you think it will do for your children. If you don't have a clear picture, how can the kids understand what is happening? At times, traditions carry us on without us taking the time to connect to the practices themselves.

As you read on, you will relate these stories to ones that are similar to those in your faith tradition, and you will be prepared to mark those moments. I am using Baptism as an example. You will be able to transpose these ideas into what you need for your own religious experience. The power of intention leads in unlocking the essence of the happening.

Baptism

At one traditional Lutheran baptism, the church adds embellishments from the women of the congregation to further support and sustain the family during this treasured time.

Blankie, Candle and Cloth

A local Lutheran church has designed a wonderful tradition for when their congregants' babies are baptized. When a member of the church is expecting a child, a ladies group gets together to make a "blankie" for the baby. It is fabricated with loving stitches long before the child comes into the world. The baby is being anticipated by the churchwomen. They are already bonded to the child before the birth or baptism. The church also gives a large candle to the family and a hand-woven napkin used for wiping the water off the head of the baby during the sacrament.

The pastor invites the family to relive the ceremony of baptism each year on its anniversary. Since the children are usually quite young, the decision to be baptized is made by the parents for them. If the family makes a tradition of lighting the candle each year, bringing out the napkin and quilt, looking through the photos, the child will learn that her baptism was important. She can then begin to take ownership of the ceremony that was done earlier on her behalf. The parents are giving the message that baptism is worthy of celebrating each year.

Our next story gives another angle of how a family designed a way to have a keepsake for the baptized child. Read about what they created and how they went about making it happen.

Welcome to the Family

Pam and Mark had a baby, named Danny. When Danny was two months old, Pam's family had a reunion. The new parents asked Grandpa, who is a minister, to baptize the baby. The occasion took place at our home, and I felt I wanted to do something special for this new little family.

I thought about the parents. Pam is somewhat quiet, very attached to the family, and likes to feel connected. Mark has felt comfortable with his family by marriage and enjoys being with the sometimes-raucous group. The family itself is close and has a tendency for pranks and laughter, but also has a side that can be more serious. Grandpa and I worked together to develop a program for the evening.

Grandpa offered the ceremony of the baptism. I bought a large green candle and decorated it with raffia and dried flowers. When the celebration began, Pam was asked to light the Danny candle, symbolizing his light being added to that of our family. Grandpa held Danny as he went around the circle of people and let each person touch the baby and say a word of welcome. When it was time for the family to affirm their position in care-taking Danny's spiritual life, those who wanted to were asked to light a candle and place it around the large one. The visible signs of the lights surrounding Danny's candle allowed each of us to see how much support there was.

After the more formal ceremony was over, the family had the opportunity to offer a personal token of welcome to Danny. I had sent out an earlier email asking family members to bring an offering to put into a scrapbook for him. This was the time to present the pages, wishes, or words of welcome. One family had designed a page that symbolized some of the family tradi-tions. Great-grandma gave a card in which she expressed her emotions of having a new great-grandson. A cousin wrote a beautiful letter explaining to Danny some of the values of the family. I found a photo of when Grandpa had baptized Pam and her cousin. In the photo were many of the same family members, although it was twenty-eight years later.

Danny was gracefully accepted as a member of our family as well as affirmed as a child of God. By sharing this experience, those present already sensed a special bonding with the baby. We all expressed our welcome to him and to his parents. Each new person who enters a family—be it by marriage or birth—changes the dynamics of the group. To have this change witnessed and acknowledged is a powerful way to connect. I know that Pam and Mark felt an increased closeness to those present and could tell that everyone in the family would be available to assist them if they ever needed extra help or support. Witnessing a baptism can be a powerful experience. The act of speaking and participating in the event helps an individual take on ownership, rather than being a passive observer.

Take ownership of your event. Put your heart into it and create a gathering to remember.

Any of these example stories take a certain amount of imagination to produce. As we have few role models, whatever new tradition we create may help others to try something new and different for themselves.

Spiritual Support

The time arrived for Terry and Tim's new baby, Shawn, to be baptized. They wanted this day to be special for them, their other children, family and close church friends. Even though Shawn was the center figure, he was too young to know what was going on. The celebration would be for the adults and older children. How could they celebrate after the church service was over?

They talked about what this meant to them and why they were doing it. They decided that when Shawn came into the world, he arrived in the secular realm. The baptism would welcome him into God's world. His parents were making the choice for him to be received into the life of the church. The family and friends would be making the decision to uphold him in his spiritual growth—probably in the church— but perhaps otherwise if he made later decisions on his own. The baptism is a public declaration of intent. Often times the members of the church are also asked to be part of the support team for the child.

Besides having a small reception for people who would be most likely to follow his spiritual growth, was there something else they could do to honor this time— something to connect them all? Terry checked on the Internet for ideas and she could find no models for what she had in mind. She then looked to the Mark the Moment recipe and was able to create a gathering time that was significant for them.

Terry had the intent to celebrate the baptism beyond the church walls. She and Tim talked about what this ceremony meant for them. What they desired was a con- necting time.

They decided to invite those who would be probably be the principles in Shawn's spiritual journey—siblings, grandparents, several aunts and uncles, and a close couple from their church—a group of about twelve. They met after brunch and sat in a circle (of course) and asked the questions: "Why is your spiritual life important to you? Why do we need to raise Shawn in this setting? Has being a part of the family a God made a difference to you?" These are interesting questions and seldom asked.

A lovely yellow candle decorated with stars and sparkles rested in the center of a table placed in the circle. Shawn's baptismal certificate and a Bible, symbols of his unfolding divine path, lay next to the candle. Each person choosing to speak would have a chance to hold Shawn as they did.

Aunt Pam started out by telling a little of her personal faith journey. She had attended Sunday school as a young person, which was fun and she learned basic morals and Bible stories. As a young woman she was less interested in spending time in a traditional church setting, in fact she didn't have any spiritual practice until she was about thirty-five, when she lost her mother. That experience encouraged her to look at life and death issues and the meaning of it all. She then reconnected with her church roots and began to explore her spiritual side, which had been neglected. She was still working on this faith journey within the structure of her church.

Tim told about never being in a church as a child. He knew some of his friends attended, but didn't realize what it was all about, as he had no experience because his family didn't attend, nor did they talk about "churchy" or spiritual matters at all. He had always felt a void in his heart but didn't know where it came from. In college, he attended an interfaith meeting and began the long process of filling in the gaps of his spiritual life—the hole in his heart was beginning to fill with love and meaning. He wanted to make sure that Shawn had the opportunity to be part of a supportive community for the spiritual part of his life.

And more stories emerged. None of the family had ever talked about anything like this. They were a little tentative about getting started, but understood that how they felt would and could make a difference in Shawn's life, as they were his support team for growing up. An incredible binding took place as these people unlocked stories from their hearts.

At the end, Terry thanked everyone for coming and gave them each a mini-version of Shawn's candle to take home with them.

Terry and Tim took the extra step to figure out how to mark this moment for Shawn, and they all benefitted from the experience. Courage to try something new was necessary, and they met the challenge.

Confirmation

Confirmation is a sacrament in the Christian Church when a person, typically a young adult, is received into the congregation. Each student is usually required to attend classes for a specific amount of time to learn about the church. When they are ready, there is a celebration to receive them into the membership. The child confirms the vows the parents made when she was baptized. She has decided that indeed, this is what she chooses now that she is old enough to make her own decisions. The scenario is a bit different if an adult is going through the process of confirmation, yet the intention remains the same.

The church, in this story, has developed some special ways to honor their confirmands. I like these ideas as they help make the celebration personal as well as honoring the entire confirmation class.

Church Welcome

A local Lutheran church has developed a lovely tradition for honoring the young people who are making the decision to be confirmed—that is, to join their church. Prior to the actual Confirmation, the group of youths has an overnight retreat. Parents organize a group of friends, teachers, relatives and mentors of the confirmand, asking each person to write a letter of affirmation. These letters are collected and put into an envelope. They are presented to each student at the end of the retreat.

They are not read during the weekend, but are for the kids to read in private.

As part of the confirmation service, each student is given a special Bible verse that has been picked out by the pastor. They are to read the verse in front of the church congregation, as well as do a short interpretation of what it means to them. The parents are asked to write about their child in a personal way—what their dreams are for the life and faith of their child. The parents then read their statements at the service. The pastor says this is the longest service of the year, one of most meaningful, and that many boxes of Kleenex are required. The students are loved and cared for, and this big step is of their own choice. This church congregation has made it clear that confirmation is a big deal as demonstrated by their actions of support and love throughout the process of taking the classes, retreating, including friends and family, and celebrating at the actual church service.

Not only are the young adults in this example confirmed in the church setting, but they are asked to figure out how to put their faith into action

Confirmation Message in Action

.

A mainstream Protestant church, which is socially active, wants to help its young adults understand that activism is intrinsic in being a member in their church family. As part of the confirmation plan, the teens spend some of their preparation looking at their community and identifying needs. As they talk about areas of concern, each young person chooses where they want to work during the week after their confirmation. They need to commit a couple of hours in service. All the pieces will be in place for them to go into the community at large, or outreach into their own church membership, to assist someone in need.

James decided to help an elderly church member take care of his garden. Sarah signed up in the elementary school to listen to children read. Mack contacted the local senior center and asked if someone needed some extra muscle for a few hours. Pam went to the local thrift store to help where needed. When these kids identified all the areas in their community that could use extra help, and realized that they were old enough to help and make a difference, they were energized and moved cheerfully into action.

At the next gathering after the workweek, the kids met and shared the stories of their experiences. They put their faith commitment into action and felt good about it.

Bar/Bat Mitzvah

In the Jewish tradition, a child becomes a responsible adult at the age of about thirteen. Until recently, only boys were honored with a Bar Mitzvah celebration. Now girls are included with a Bat Mitzvah. Depending on which synagogue, privileges and responsibilities vary. Whether for a Bar or Bat Mitzvah, the celebration means that the young person is now responsible for him/herself and for adherence to Jewish law, tradition and ethics, can participate in all areas of Jewish life and read out of the Torah. What we are celebrating is the passage into this role in the synagogue. Keeping that in mind, our stories give a couple of concrete examples of what several families have created to make this transition even more meaningful as personal touches have been added.

This story is unusual because a mother and her son decided to mark their re-entry into their faith community together. This celebration took time, effort and courage to achieve.

Mother and Son Crossing Together

Ruby reclaimed her Jewish heritage by giving herself a Bat Mitzvah at age thirty-one. When she was growing up, women weren't welcomed into the synagogue with a special ceremony at age thirteen like the boys.

When Ruby had a son of her own and was living far away from her roots, she began to think about what her Jewish background meant to her. She and her son had a close relationship and made many life decisions jointly. When Josh was ten, he and Ruby decided to learn Hebrew as a way to connect to their heritage and get ready for Josh's Bar Mitzvah. After two and a half years of study, they were ready to have a Bar Mitzvah to honor Josh's transition into manhood, and to have a Bat Mitzvah to allow Ruby an opportunity to publicly reclaim her religious roots.

They searched for a Rabbi to assist them on their mission and were given permission to design what they needed, as long as it included a teacher, the community and readings from the Torah. Ruby looked long and hard for a Torah she could borrow and use for the ceremony. A friend built her an ark to hold the scroll. She had problems embracing the traditional prayers from the Torah, and finally had to formulate her own to integrate the old and the new into her life. Both she and Josh wrote their own interpretations for their celebration, which were shared at the ceremony. They wanted a big party to accompany this celebration. Friends had a fundraiser to pay for a band. It was a wonderful celebration welcoming Josh as a man into the Jewish faith and Ruby's re-connection with her heritage.

The passion, dedication, and the sharing of two generations moved me in this story. Ruby had the vision to design what she wanted for herself and her son, thus creating a memorable occasion for both of them.

Read now about a family who shared stories of their Jewish heritage. By creating a place where children could listen to their elders during this significant passage, the group bonded in a new way.

Family Faith Heritage

Emil observed his Bar Mitzvah this last August. His parents planned a traditional celebration with an additional touch. After the ceremony was over and the feast was done, the family and close friends gathered for one final component. Emil had worked hard in his classes to learn all that was required.   His parents wanted to add a part where he could see, feel and understand the practical application of his new role. What does this mean? What different is going to happen? Will his life be the same even though he participated in a significant religious transition?

When the group gathered, the parents asked them to consider the question "Why is our faith tradition important?" They took some moments of silence to think, as it wasn't something they thought about every day. The center table held his mom's shawl, his dad's Torah, Emil's certificate and a candle symbolizing his new role.

Finally, Uncle Dan said he appreciated the opportunity to speak on this subject. He talked about his father and what the faith tradition had meant to their family as their persecution escalated in Russia. He told about the strength it took to remove the entire family to a new location where they could be free to practice their faith.

Grandma Alice talked about how she wished she could have had a celebration like this when she was a young girl. When she was young, the passage was only recognized for the boys. Fortunately times have changed in modern America and girls are also honored as members of the synagogue and have the same rites as the men.

Emil's dad told about how in times of struggle, when he thought he couldn't continue on, the strength of his faith and the support of the community upheld him until he got his feet on the ground. Without this extra foundation and spiritual support, his life might have been changed.

Stories poured out, strengthening the convictions of everyone, because they were witnessing the effects of what the traditions could hold. Emil received another level of appreciation of his heritage and realized how this could be an important factor in his life choices. The celebration centered on Emil, yet all present gained insight into each other and their spiritual journeys. Emil's parents created a place to hear these personal accounts. They were also taking a risk, as there was the possibility that no one would speak at the gathering, yet they trusted that the process would work and were willing to try.

After reading these examples of religious transitions, please note the deep traditions that form the basis of these celebrations. Each family builds on the history of their faith and adds a dimension of personal expression to the established form. The long-standing practices connect us with the power of our past. Yet we need to be responsible for making the experience personal and applicable in the present day for it to be meaningful and valid. Looking into the history of the event, taking time to decide why we are choosing to celebrate, clarifying the intent and making it personal offer the ingredients for an exceptional experience.

The stories tell of rites of passage within the religious community. Even if you are not a part of such a community, you may want to look for an opportunity when children and young adults move through an important stage. Coming of age moments come in many packages. Being discerning and knowing your child will help you decide when appropriate action might be taken: from overcoming a challenge, moving through puberty, obtaining a driver's license, to understanding a parental divorce. Life presents rich change that can act as a catalyst for a beginning, if it is but acknowledged.

Take these samples and add them to your supply of ideas. The more ideas you have handy, the easier it is to invent what you need when the time comes.

Wedding Celebrations: Showering Treasures of the Heart

Weddings and wedding showers may seem like times in life when a meaningful moment is created by the event itself. Many of us have been to weddings and showers and know that not all of them are created equal. What makes the difference? Is there a way that we can add a dimension of heart and depth to an existing institution? These examples may help you recognize the difference.

This is a great story as it tells about showering more than the bride. When the guests left this shower, they all felt affirmed, enlightened, motivated and uplifted. You, too, can create such a setting for yourself. Read on to find out how this was achieved.

Showering Wisdom

Mary's daughter, Molly, was preparing to be married. The usual frenzy ensued. Who should be invited? The space was limited. Location? Caterer? Flowers? Music? All the customary elements needed to be addressed for this momentous event to take place. Mary looked deeply into herself and asked the question "What is it that I would like to send with this precious daughter of mine, as she embarks on a new life journey of marriage and partnership?"

Years ago when Mary got married, people didn't talk about the challenges that most couples face in a committed relationship. One was married and lived happily ever after—even when the divorce statistics prove otherwise. Mary decided to gather a group of women who would be willing to meet with Molly and address the question, "What is it that has sustained you during your marriage/partnership/relationship when the going got tough?" As this specific question revealed itself, she then moved into the next phase of planning. Who would come? When? Where? How?

Mary discussed the basic plan with Molly, but not the details, as she wanted some of it to be a surprise. She needed Molly's approval of the idea, especially the question, before moving forward. The shower date was for 11 a.m. on a Saturday morning about a month before the wedding. The place was Mary's home where Molly grew up. The sixteen women invited were those most connected to Molly throughout her growing up years. Some had many years of marriage experience. A few were single. Several had been divorced. Most were Mary's age—old enough to be Molly's mother. A few were younger to balance the scale.

Mary mailed out invitations with "the question" included. The invitation left the door open about how to respond. One woman, who was out of town, sent Molly a letter to be read during the shower. Her grandmother, who lived far away, sent a message because she wanted to be included.

Since the shower was planned for the late morning, Mary decided to make tea sandwiches—lots of those little old fashioned open-face ones with cucumbers, egg salad and salmon spread. This was kind of unusual, because Mary is not normally an old-fashioned teatime person. Yet her intuition kept prodding her in this direction. She also made individual little cakes from her grandmother's recipe. Mimosas and coffee rounded out the menu. The stage was set with food.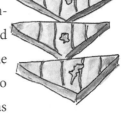

The day arrived and the living room chairs were set in a circle. Many of the women were rather nervous about the procedure, as they hadn't experienced such a gathering before—no gifts, just bring their experience and a willingness to share what might be a treacherous subject.

A little purple stone heart was used as a talking piece and would be given to Molly when this gathering was over. Since each woman held this heart, it held the energy of everyone present. The morning opened with a "practice circle," or "check-in" circle, to get settled. The first round was to state your name, tell how you were connected to the bride, and how many years of marriage experience you brought to this group. Wonderful stories emerged from this opening time as women shared about their relationships with Molly. All were moved at the interconnections within the group and how loved and supported Molly was in her home community. The years of collective marriage wisdom brought to this group were added up. The group was drawing from more than three hundred years of marriage experience! The importance of an opening circle is to let people hear their own voices, feel connected to the group and be at ease with the process.

In the second round, each guest spoke to "the question." The little, purple heart became warmer and warmer as it circulated around the group. Some advice was offered, but most of the words of wisdom came from the voice of personal experience. One woman crocheted a gorgeous bag in which she added a few treasures that symbolized some of the messages of marriage.

As Mary talked to Molly later about this experience and what had stayed with her, she mentioned an overwhelming feeling of support and closeness. Many of these women had already supported her through her growing years, and now they were ready to launch her into the next step of marriage. She also said that she felt this group would be a resource for her if she reached a place of needing help with her relationship. Molly felt great comfort in that realization.

There is a little sub-story that goes with this shower. Beth, mother of the groom, belongs to a book club. When she mentioned the impending shower to her book club, the group recognized the importance of the question. They were planning a retreat together and decided to talk about the question among themselves. While shopping on their trip, one of them found an "Advice Jar." Knowing that advice isn't exactly wisdom, though the thought was close enough—the women who didn't even know Molly—added their words to the jar that Beth presented at the shower. Other women also mentioned how exploring this question had encouraged them to think about their relationships and talk about it with important members of their family.

This story shows us a symbolic way for friends to stay connected when a life change may separate the participants.

Ribbons at the Wedding Shower

Susan was getting married and her friends planned a shower for her. At the shower, the hostess, Kate, started the gathering by asking each person present to say what she loved and appreciated about Susan. Kate had brought yards and yards of ribbon, which she had saved, scrounged and bought for the occasion. The speaking order was based on birth dates. The earliest date in January started, and the next closest birthday to her date followed. The first person took one end of the ribbon and held it while she spoke. She kept the ribbon when she was finished, and it was stretched to wherever the next speaker was seated. Thus the ribbon meandered around the room and among the group. The web of ribbon finished at the last speaker. When this opening sequence was finished, it was as if this could have been the entire shower activity. Susan was filled with joy at the affirmations and love given to her by her close friends. She saved the ribbon and used it during many of the following wedding festivities, including it in the rehearsal dinner and at the wedding itself. She wanted to be reminded of the wonderful opening of the heart for her—of the opportunity people took to honor her in her time of transition.

Here's another simple to plan, and easy to participate in, celebration. You can use this appreciation circle either with flowers or candles for many occasions. People don't seem to get tired of being a part of the contributing circle or to be the recipient.

Affirming the Bride

A wedding was being planned. The groom was an only child from a divorced family where the mom worked valiantly to support the two of them during his childhood. The bride was the youngest of a large family. She was the first to go to college. She left home at a young age to seek her own life without the restrictions of her family.

The bride and the groom's families were having difficulties communicating about celebrating this special day and union. The mother of the groom decided she wanted to create something special for the bride to help her feel welcome and worthy as she moved into her new life with her partner. One family was full of professional facilitators. One family had a hard time talking to each other, let alone anyone else. This situation was going to take some delicate maneuvering to create a gathering that would work for all involved.

Once the intention was clear—to help the bride feel accepted, deserving and cared for by friends and family—then the actual planning could start. A bridesmaid was preparing a traditional shower for the bride. The groom's mother felt this would be the spot to insert a little meaningful moment. Since the families were so diverse, it was decided that to do something too far from the norm would not be appropriate. The plan was that the shower would be traditional, as planned by the maid of honor. After the packages were open, the groom's mom would offer an appreciation circle. Each person was asked to bring a flower to the shower. An empty vase was placed in the center of the circle. People were invited to tell the bride what they saw that she was bringing to the marriage. As each person made her verbal presentation, she placed her flower in the vase. By the time each person had a chance to speak, the vase was filled with lovely flowers that represented the bride's qualities. She was wrapped in the positive energy that all the family members brought to her. This circle helped bind the group, rather than dwell on their differences. After all, everyone wanted the wedding couple to start their marriage as blessed as possible. Affirming the bride put everyone on common ground, and the families began the process of appreciating each other.

The following project turned out to be fun, creative, inclusive, different and memorable. Using the unique circumstances of the wedding, we were able to create this festive bonding of guests before the actual wedding. I am sure you will find yourself smiling when you read this one!

This Is Your Life

On the weekend of our daughter's wedding, many out-of-town friends arrived to join the festivities. Many didn't know each other, because they came from all parts of the country. Our daughter, Melissa, asked her dad to design an activity which would act as a bonding time for the group of nearly twenty special friends. Most of the guests arrived on Friday evening. The wedding was held on Sunday evening. The time slot allowed for a connecting activity was to be on Saturday morning from 9-1. Jim, Melissa's dad, decided to do a mini "This is Your Life" experience about Melissa and Ryan, as the couple had grown up together and had known each other since the age of three.

All convened at nine in the morning and headed for the local high school that both the bride and groom attended, passing the elementary and middle schools on the way. Ryan's science teacher met them there and gave them a school tour. One of Ryan's significant experiences during high school was participating in a bridge building contest. His teacher was the advisor and assisted Ryan as he competed at the local, regional and onto the national level. Jim built a wooden bridge similar to the ones the students had built, which he brought along to the school. In the contest, the bridge that holds the heaviest weight be- fore it breaks wins the contest. The instructor  had the weights out to break Jim's bridge, re- enacting Ryan's contest.

The next stop featured Melissa. One of her big high school activities was being in Pony Club and competing her horse, Bidley, who was still living with us. Jim asked me to saddle him up and get him ready for all the guests to ride. We set up a mini-obstacle course and anyone who wanted to ride was given an opportunity to try. Many had never ridden a horse before, and Bidley acted as the perfect gentleman for the occasion.

After the ride, the group moved down to our local marina. Melissa had grown up around boats all her life. Our family had a trawler in which we spent many happy moments cruising the local waters. Jim asked me to make a picnic for the group, and off they went for a lunch cruise.

By the time the morning was over, the group had experienced several shared activities, had time to talk to each other, become acquainted, and had a taste of Melissa and Ryan's growing-up world. Saturday evening, we had the out-of-towners to our home for dinner, which furthered the acquaintanceships. By the time of the wedding on Sunday, the guests were clearly enjoying each other's company.

From the intention of creating a situation that would encourage connecting, Jim examined the lives of the bride and groom. He chose activities that would tell something about them as they grew up together on our island and offering experiences where the guests could participate. There was time to chat as the group moved around to the various locations. The shared experience created new memories. Jim understood the intention. He looked carefully at the two people who were involved, and what needed to happen grew out of those criteria. The participants, as well as the bride and groom, had a great time and meaningful moments were created for all.

This unique story encourages each of us to recognize our inner guidance. This incredible resource is available to all who take the time to identify and trust this gift from the Universe. In our story, Kathy felt she had to act upon her dream as it was a clear directive and here is how it turned out.

A Garden Shower

This is an important story, not only because of the resulting wedding shower, but because a woman had enough courage to act on her vision. Kathy's only daughter, Jess, was planning her wedding. Kathy is a thoughtful and quiet person who is very connected to her children. Some weeks prior to the wedding, Kathy had a dream about a shower for Jess. The dream was so detailed that it showed the location of the shower, indicated the guest list and what the guests were to bring to the shower. As I was invited to this occasion, I have a first-hand report of the event. Initially, Kathy didn't know what to do with this vivid dream. She wrote down all the details in the morning after having it, so that she would remember. She finally decided that she needed to act on it.

This is where I feel the power of this story comes for all of us. How often do we have inspirational ideas which may come from night dreams, daydreams, thoughts generated while we are walking in the woods or on the beach, or when we are talking to a friend. Having these ideas is not such an unusual situation. What makes this story special is that Kathy made the decision to act upon her inspiration. I want this story to remind us that we, too, can trust our intuition, our inner self, and our subconscious, whatever we call it, to move into action. Take these hints seriously as our internal wisdom is being accessed. We receive our ideas in diverse and interesting ways. We need to acknowledge and act upon them with courage.

The guests received a lovely invitation in the mail from Kathy. It was printed on paper with a beautiful garden theme border. It invited us to tea under the large locust tree in Kathy's yard on a chosen afternoon. Each guest was asked to bring a verbal offering to Jess on a particular subject. Each subject and the presenter were mentioned in the dream. I was asked to speak about marriage.

Twelve women met under the tree. There were small tables covered with tablecloths, a particular kind of tea, which was also indicated in the dream, along with little cookies and sandwiches. The guests sat in a circle surrounding Jess. She was wrapped in a shawl. People spoke to Jess on their subject. I was rather intimidated about talking about marriage, yet I was able to move beyond my own inhibitions to offer what I could. It was a lesson on trusting myself and having the courage to do what was asked. The entire shower encouraged the guests to move beyond themselves to offer to Jess wisdom, information, love and advice that needed to come from that particular person at that particular time. As in most cases, what started out to be an honoring and supporting of Jess moving into her marriage, turned into being a time of deep-heart connection for all involved. The setting was full of trust and respect. The women knew they could reveal what was coming up from the well deep within them.

Remember this story when you feel an intuitive hit. Don't dismiss it as outrageous or ridiculous. Something inside you has prompted this idea. Take courage and heart, and package it where it needs to go. You are asked to be the guide and lead the way.

This simple and straightforward idea presented itself after a look into the family structure. This more reserved group needed an activity that would not intimidate them, yet allow each person to participate. We were able to create just the right happening.

My Father Is Getting Married

Lindsay's dad was getting married. He is in his seventies. His wife had died and his family had been in disarray for some years. Lindsay talked to me about what she might do to welcome her dad's fiancée, Jeanette, into their family. The intention was clear.

Lindsay and I talked about her family, their values, and their comfort level of speaking in a group, so I could get a sense of what might work for them. A family dinner was planned for the evening before the wedding. This would be the time to offer an activity or celebration. I told Lindsay about the appreciation/birthday circle using the bowl of rice and candles. We also talked about giving each person a flower and putting an empty vase beside Jeanette. We then thought of how Jeanette would probably be providing meals for the family from time to time, and perhaps they could include a favorite recipe, so should she would know what everyone liked. That idea struck a chord with Lindsay. Jeanette would feel like she was being let in on some intimate family details by sharing the recipes.

Afterwards, as she told me about the ceremony of welcome, Lindsay's face was glowing. Every person had contributed a verbal welcome—even the five-year-old great-grandchild—a recipe for the box, and an explanation of why they picked that particular recipe. Jeanette kept wondering where the idea had come from and was

FAMILY RECIPES

thrilled at the outpouring of acceptance and love coming from her new family. The participants seemed glad to have a time and place to express to Jeanette how they were feeling at this auspicious time of change for them all.

Lindsay knew about the letting go part. She offered the celebration in good faith with a heart full of appreciation and love for this woman who was giving her dad a new outlook on life. She knew she was taking a risky step in asking for the time to do something different. The family's usual style was to meet for dinner, eat, and then go their separate ways. Creating an activity where all could participate was an unusual concept. By keeping the question straightforward and simple, providing a personal recipe, and seeing the box fill with cards as well as the wishes that went with them, the family bonded and shared what would become a special memory for all. It also started the wedding weekend off to a positive beginning, as Jeanette was a bit nervous about how she was being viewed and accepted.

This bride and groom put their heads together to honor their faith traditions, family traditions and newfound joint interests to design a distinctive celebration. This is their story, but you can use their process and be inspired to look with new eyes to whatever it is you are called to help produce. You can do it for yourself or assist another. Be courageous and trust your ingenuity at a new level.

A Fresh Look at a Wedding

As I was talking with my daughter, Melissa, about her wedding, she reminded me of something that may be significant for this part of the book. I had not thought to include weddings themselves, as they seem to stand alone for creating meaningful moments. Melissa received so much positive feedback about her wedding, saying that it was personal and that the couple had shared so much of themselves in the process that I have decided to include some of what they chose to do. What I would like to address is the intention of the wedding, so this might encourage some of you to look beyond the traditional.

Melissa's grandfather, who was also the minister for this wedding, met with the bride and groom ahead of the event to discuss plans. He suggested to them that they were inviting guests to the wedding and to seriously consider that issue. A guest is more than a witness. A guest is a person to whom they are offering hospitality. How do you want to treat a guest? How would you like to be treated? He also suggested that they might want to make the event something personal—to have the courage to add their personal touches—to move beyond the standard traditional formats available through various church denominations.

With these two intentions paving the path, the bride and groom worked at making their weekend unique and welcoming. If you have read the story earlier in this chapter about "This is Your Life," you will have an idea of the way that Melissa's father helped the guests become acquainted. We also found small houses where the guests could stay, where they would have more of a chance to interact. Without that intention of honoring the guests, I doubt if the housing and the activity would have happened.

At the actual ceremony, the couple took the role, which the minister/priest/rabbi usually takes, of extending the welcome to the guests who came from all over the country to share in this special day. They asked two friends to speak at the ceremony. They risked a little chaos and let them prepare whatever it was that they wanted to say—as opposed to asking them to read a specific passage. This added a very personal touch and freshness to the occasion, as no one knew what was going to be said. The bride and groom each prepared personal statements about what they wanted to say about their partner—what they loved about them, what attracted them to each other. This turned out to be a very intimate glimpse into their love and their relationship. They hadn't read these to each other before, so it was new for all of us. We guests witnessed a special pouring forth from the heart. We felt honored to be included in this touching moment. Later in the ceremony, grandpa took over and discharged his ministerial duties and the service concluded.

At the reception, all guests were introduced, which took a few minutes, but helped everyone get the connections of who was who. The mother of the groom hand-dyed all the tablecloths and napkins for the reception. She had also made purple beads by hand, that were added to napkin ring holders with little silver bicycles and violins symbolizing the couple. Guests were invited to take home the napkin rings as a gift, and also a votive candle, which was at each place-setting.

I feel drawn to offer this example of a wedding because so many people mentioned its uniqueness and how good the guests felt about this ceremony and reception. Every part of the wedding had personal touches. The point is, when you are beginning to plan a wedding, start with intention. Each intention will spell out a different way to design the day. It takes courage to do something out of the ordinary. If a traditional ceremony is what makes you comfortable, do it with purpose, but don't do something just because it's "what's always done." Be willing to embrace your dreams and desires by setting your intention, then allowing the magic to work as your create your exceptional day.

Adoption: New Beginnings

My friend, Brenda, has helped me become aware of the necessity of talking about honoring and creating meaningful moments around adoption issues. We are talking about lots of people here: there are the birth moms who are making the decision to turn their children over to a permanent caretaker; there are the babies themselves who have no choice in the matter; there are the new parents who are excited about the promise of a new family. The needs of each of these three groups are vitally different. When these transitions are addressed, there is a better chance for healthy exchange.

Brenda herself was adopted as a child. She eventually became a therapist and developed a practice that helped people deal with adoption issues. She has addressed and personally experienced the impact of many of the secrets that can surround adoption. She has helped me see the shame and guilt (usually from the birth mom) and the loss of control (of the baby) as creating debilitating emotional baggage if these matters are not acknowledged. Not until recently in our culture have families begun to talk freely about these issues.

Not too long ago, it was forbidden by law to give out the names of the birth parents. By being able to deal with the truth, much unhappiness and delusion can be bypassed. When a child knows and understands the circumstances through which her mom decided to give her up, she may be able to forgive her and thank her for offering her a better and more secure place in the world. When a birth mom is able to talk about what happened—even though she or her family may be ashamed—the entire family may be able to move forward, leaving the shame behind. When the action has been witnessed and named, it is possible for release and forgiveness to move into the picture. Culturally we need to move out of the secrecy and lies which surround these issues, so that healing and understanding take their place.

Brenda feels strongly that when a baby is transferred from the birth mom to the adoptive mom, all the support team should be in attendance. The baby needs to be held by the birth mom, who tells the baby about the circumstances that en-couraged her to offer this child to a new family. The new parents have an opportunity to express their delight and happiness at the prospect of having this child in their lives, and to cherish the responsibility of raising her. Even though 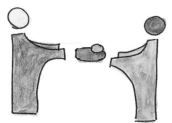 the baby may be an infant at this time, she hears and internalizes what's happening. She begins her new life with honesty and dignity as she receives the energetic emotional responses from the people in the room. This transfer of the child from one home to another creates a meaningful moment for all the parties. This doesn't mean that it is easy. It means that the transfer is understood and honored by all. In these highly emotionally charged times, it is important to create a safe place where all can express directly what they think is going on in their hearts.

If the adoption takes place overseas, variations to this basic theme of honesty and honoring will be different. Each circumstance requires unique handling. With the intention in place, the transfer of the child can be as healthy as possible for all involved.

We are talking about loss and grieving in this transition. The birth mom may be feeling shame for having gotten into the circumstance in the first place. Letting go of the child is one of the most difficult choices she will make in her life. She needs to acknowledge that grief is a part of this process.

Not many people think about the small baby during this time. She is losing her birth family through no choice of her own. She is a victim of other people's major life decisions. This child needs to be honored by having the truth as part of her heritage and roots.

When an adoptee is ready to find her birth parents, it constitutes a rite of passage. For her personal health, she needs to be supported to find her parents when she feels the time is right. She is reclaiming her lost power. She was transferred when she was powerless. Now she is going to move back into a position of power by choosing to find her biological family and to fill in the pieces of the puzzle of who she is. And of course, the biological parents need to be ready to meet their child.

In our culture, divorce is common and blended families are the rule rather than the exception. Many children have three or four sets of grandparents and several dads and moms. Over time, we, as a culture, are getting used to this scene. In the same way, we need to trust that there is room in the hearts of adopted children for all their parents and understand the different place which each holds. The act of finding a birth family is creating a meaningful moment for a child. Claiming power is important work that needs to be done for healing and understanding to overcome the shame and secrets involved in hiding adoption facts.

Culturally, we are still learning how to feel concerning these issues of adoption. In fairness to all the people involved, the intention to build new families was and is positive and loving. The skills necessary for healthy lives within the framework of adoption are still being explored and discovered. The truth just is. If we insist on adding judgment to it, we are traveling into dangerous territory. When we accept the truth for a fact, we can then move on. Hiding, without witnessing and acknowledging, offers a climate of distrust and misunderstanding. Honesty and integrity are the base of these heart matters of adoptive issues.

Read about a courageous family who worked together to make an adoption time an extraordinary experience.

A New Family

Barbara was ready to give birth to her first child. She was sixteen and in the middle of her junior year of high school. The father of the child was about the same age. When Barbara found out she was pregnant, she talked about the situation with her parents, the boyfriend, and the boyfriend's parents. All agreed that it would be in her best interest to see a counselor and get some professional perspective to help sort out what to do.

The family was able to find a reliable person to help them all. They met and discussed options. What was the best for the child? What was best for Barbara? What about the boy and his family? After this was explored, the decision was made to let the child go to a family who was ready to take on the responsibility of a new baby.

The next step was to find a place for the baby. That process was followed and a wonderful family came onto the scene. Barbara and her family became acquainted with the adoptive parents. She began to feel more and more secure about her decision. These wonderful people would be in a much better position to care for her child as she grew up. At sixteen, Barbara felt that she couldn't provide the stability and security she would prefer. She already loved this child enough to let it go to a better place than she could provide at this time.

The therapist suggested that Barbara convene the extended family at the birth site in the hospital when the baby arrived. At that time, people would be invited to speak what was in their hearts. It was a sacred and confidential space where the truth of that moment would be honored. Barbara was able to express her grief at letting go of the child. The baby's father told of his relief that his child would be well taken care of. The grandparents spoke from their perspectives. The new parents were able to talk about their joy on receiving this child and to thank Barbara for giving them the opportunity. The baby herself was participating in the process by feeling the energy and hearing the voices of the most important people in her life. From what research tells us, babies absorb feelings of the mother when they are in the womb as well as after birth. When these feelings can be expressed in a positive and loving attitude, the atmosphere for the child entering the world may be as supportive and encouraging as possible.

This ceremony, ritual, or whatever you call it, was a very unusual and gutsy move on Barbara's part. All the principals in the baby's life were present to honor the immense transition that was taking place. The charged atmosphere was diffused because all the roles were honored and emotions allowed to be expressed. The child changed from one caring family to another. When the time was right, the child will most probably take the opportunity to meet her biological parents and hopefully be able to understand the choices they made on her behalf.

This story of courage and honesty serves to inspire and to make a difficult situation take on integrity. Each adoptive situation is unique. What works for one family may not work for another. Take the formula offered in *Celebrating Beginnings and Endings* and use it for your situation. Be clear about the intention and move ahead from there. Remember to trust your inner guidance to lead you to the path to serve all involved in the highest and best way.

Traveling overseas to pick up a child for adoption offers different challenges from our previous story. The child may be older. She may be taken from a foster family or orphanage. The new parents need to tune into the situation and look carefully at appropriate actions. Read what one family did to honor their adoption transition.

Overseas Adoption

Dana and Steve had finally jumped through enough hoops to receive clearance to adopt a baby girl from Thailand. Her name was Melody and she had been living in an orphanage for some time. She was about two years old. They were very excited about the event and were going to travel to Thailand to pick her up. They thought a lot about this transition for her to a real family, a new culture, an airplane ride and all the changes this young one would be asked to make. What could they do to ease this transition for her? How could they help her keep her roots, even though she was leaving her country of origin?

Dana felt, at the very least, they could keep a record of their trip. It would be like her birth book—a variation on the theme due to unusual circumstances. Dana bought a nice scrapbook, brought along scissors, glue and other assorted odds and ends that might make the scrapbooking creative, fun and appeal to a kid. She started right away on the airplane from Seattle, describing the trip, and their excitement and nervousness at picking up Melody and becoming parents.

When they arrived at the orphanage, they took pictures of the caretakers. These were the women in Melody's life who had become her surrogate parents until her new situation was established. They were her family to that point, and were important to her. Dana saved every little item of interest and pasted it in the book. She described the details of the orphanage, so that perhaps one day Melody might remember her Thai roots. They took little trips around the region while all the paperwork was finished, and Dana put all those places in the book as well.

The scrapbook became a treasure, as well as an account of Melody's trip to America. When we first met her at about age four, Dana brought the book along so Melody could show us. She was proud of it and excited that she had a story to tell. Dana and Steve had done a great job at smoothing the transition from one country to another, from one household to another, and honoring all that transpired for each of them. This was Melody's personal story, and she was eager to share it with anyone who would listen.

Now that you have stepped through the portal of wonder and can recognize the positive energy that you can infuse into life, capture these moments. With pencil in hand, keep notes in the margins of people, places and occasions that long to be noticed. Use this book as an ongoing guide, collecting ideas that you can return to later on and put into practice. Keep it handy as you don't know when inspiration will strike and you will want these gems handy for later use.

Part II: Transitions
Embracing Change

TROPICAL AMERICAS

Transitions are endings and beginnings—something is shifting within your world. You can decide if and how you want to accept this movement. The loss usually comes first, and with some time and assistance, you realize that a new fresh start is on the horizon. This section chooses five common life events that encourage or require adjustment. Of course, there are many more of them, but if you read these examples, apply the recipe to your situation, you will be on the road to smoothly traversing the choppy water. When you recognize a life change, you are ready to embrace it, as opposed to fighting it. The stories provide insights and underscore the courage of folks who recognized change and moved into action, being proactive in a situation they may or may not have asked for.

Empty Nest: The Children are Gone

For most families, having the last child leave home requires adjustment. So many years have been devoted to raising the children that the emotional space left behind seems enormous. Great amounts of time and energy expended on the kids are now available for the parents. What can they do to fill this void? As each of us is different, this transition can go seamlessly as parents have the opportunity to reconnect with each other, or they can wallow in the unrest that follows, or they can acknowledge the shift by channeling the energy in another direction. Read what a few people have done to mark the change and allow the void to slowly fill with good wishes, good will and healthy change.

The following project took a lot of work, which turned out to be part of the gift of the task. Barbara needed to throw herself into something significant to use her unsettled energy This wonderful legacy for her daughter and the rest of the family resulted from her effort.

Barbara's Cookbook

Barbara's daughter, Karin, was ready to leave home. Barbara was facing an empty nest. She sensed the magnitude of this passage before it happened. She wanted to do something to honor this change for herself and Karin.

Dorm life, roommates, college classes and new friends sparked Karin's desire to leave home, and she was eager to move out into the world. Even though Barbara was excited for her daughter and her new adventures, she looked at this change with mixed feelings—excited for her daughter to grow up and make her way in the world, and aware that the family dynamics would change. Most of all, Barbara would miss Karen's daily presence.

Barbara thought about what she might create to honor this passage. Karin had many friends, but a party was not going to fill the need. Barbara realized she wanted her project to be more intimate. She looked into herself to see what she might be able to offer Karin that was a unique expression of herself, her values and family.

During the process of thinking about the project, Barbara remembered that she loves to cook and is the keeper of the family stories. The thought of creating a cookbook for Karin ignited her energy. In the book, she would compile favorite family recipes and tell where they came from. She would insert family lore so that Karin would preserve the record of their traditions.

Barbara worked hard collecting recipes and stories. She talked to her siblings for additional reminders of her own childhood. She contacted an Internet company that specializes in making books. She sent the material to the company and they sent back a finished product for not too much money. This was a huge undertaking, yet Barbara was ready, and almost needed to put her energy into this big project. It helped diffuse the angst that she felt when she thought of Karin leaving. By the time Karin was presented with the book, Barbara felt contentment and satisfaction. She had put her anxiety into a productive endeavor that supported her during the transition and gave Karin a practical gift from the heart.

I find this story interesting in that the needs of both parties are more evident than in some of our stories. Karin wants to spread her wings and fly. Barbara wants to acknowledge the empty nest. Designing the cookbook as a tool for keeping them connected is a satisfying solution for this challenge. It uses Barbara's interest and talents, and sends them along with Karin.

This story tells of a woman who uses a unique opportunity combined with a long time dream to ease her transition. As you look into yourself and look around you, sometimes when things look bleak, a new and encouraging picture emerges which infuses life with joy and even daring.

Empty Nest, Full Pasture

Nancy and her husband raised two daughters. They also had horses, which gave them all pleasure. It meant a lot of work, but the girls were responsible and took care of that. Saddles, clothing, a trailer, and a place to keep the horses in the back yard—everything was in place for them to ride. The sport kept the girls busy, active and out of trouble.

Nancy was a substitute teacher during the time that the girls were growing up, so she could be around home when they were riding and keep an eye on them. When the youngest daughter went off to college, Nancy retired from subbing—but what now? She would take some time to explore options for the next phase of her life journey.

Meanwhile, Nancy realized that she had the time and interest to start riding herself. At age forty-five, she had hardly ever been on a horse, yet dreamed of horses and riding all her growing-up years. Nancy thought seriously about what this would mean for her. By adding stable chores as well as the riding to her day, she would stay active and outside. She could tune into her body in a new way by learning how to stay balanced in the saddle. She could finally fulfill this lifelong dream of dancing with a horse. Yes, it was time-consuming and would keep her tied down because the horses needed daily care, yet her spirit could soar while she continued to explore her professional options.

After seriously looking at what all this might mean, Nancy decided to go ahead and give it a try. The rest of this adventure is another story in itself.

I applaud the courage of this middle-aged woman to follow a dream and to use the opportunity that was literally in her backyard. She marked her moment of transition from mothering her children to mothering herself by allowing her fantasy to become a reality. Whether or not she kept riding isn't important. Nancy seized her moment and embraced it fully.

When becoming aware of intention, magic can happen. It arrives in many sorts of packages, which adds to the mystery. Trust the process. Open your heart and imagination. Off you go into a world of wonder.

This unusual story comes from my own experience, but I have also heard similar ones from others. Even last night I was talking to my brother-in-law and he was experiencing the same sort of "in between time" before knowing where to move on.

Patience for Inspiration

When our daughters left home, I retired from teaching. I was just in my mid-forties. I knew that my teaching vocation had been perfect for the years when my priorities were raising children. I also could feel that there was more to come in my life, even if I wasn't sure what it was. The empty nest was stimulating me to move on to my next phase—to reinvent myself in some way, but what?

My intention was to figure out this next step. I had been so busy with kids and getting through the daily challenges of life that I hadn't taken the time to pursue other avenues of expression or passion. I wanted to continue my life with purpose.

I needed to move into the exploration phase. As I look back on it, I realize that this piece took almost four years. Patience was part of my growing edge. I gave myself permission to follow any trail that piqued my interest: go to a movie, read a book, go to a lecture, try some silent introspection, take a class . . . whatever was out there to help expand my horizons.

I think one reason that the process took so long was that I was tired. I had given so much of myself to the children's rearing time that I needed to recharge my internal batteries before I could launch into something that would demand my attention and effort. I think that sometimes we don't realize that we can be as depleted as we are—especially women who are also going through physical changes in menopause, which can start in the forties. We keep blundering through life and then wondering why the sky is falling around us. I guess I was lucky that I instinctively understood that I needed this time to reevaluate before I could move on. I don't mean to say that I only did soul-scarching for four years. Life goes on, yet my internal focus was on this intention of uncovering my next path.

When the exploration path seemed to be winding down, the pieces started to fall into place and a plan emerged. I needed a little encouragement from the Universe in the forms of special people to validate me, which helped me move ahead.

I'm sharing my story, but this is about the process. Your story will surface when you follow the recipe. You must trust the process and you may be surprised and delighted, as I was, to what might happen.

I was always interested in medicine when I was growing up, but decided that the lifestyle wasn't a good fit for me. I followed my family tradition for teaching, which is buried deep in my bones. A friend gave me the book *Women's Bodies, Women's Wisdom* by Dr. Christiane Northrup (Bantam, 1994) and that shook my world. I was fascinated with the scientific concepts she presented underlined with rich intuitive trusting and courage to take back personal power when confronting medical issues. About that same time, some other friends encouraged me to take a training called Peerspirit (Christina Baldwin and Ann Linnea), which offers facilitation skills. If I hadn't read the book, then allowed myself to take the training, my life would have been different. The training packaged my teaching skills with facilitation skills, so I felt I could offer a space where women could talk over intense and critical issues of health. As the impression of my vision grew, I found I was merging my interest in our bodies with my quest for learning. I began to develop classes for women who wanted to explore the relationship between their minds, bodies and spirits. Another friend pushed me into the starting box and I was finally off—recharged from emotional rest and ready to tackle what was next.

The rest of the story unfolds as I facilitated classes, offered retreats, set up a website, and started this book—none of these things were on my radar as potential future life experiences, yet I found my calling and purpose. How can we turn our backs to that message?

As I was talking with my brother-in-law, he was explaining how he was taking the time to redefine himself and priorities since his daughters and wife had left. He had a fulfilling job, but also realized that there was more for him "out there." He works as a volunteer for a business that helps people start their own companies. He actively follows leads that show up on his personal radar. He has made a short-term goal of doing one random act of kindness each day to see how that feels, while the bigger task unfolds. He is essentially undertaking a similar exploring process.

As we live longer, our senior brains and health are better than at any time in history. We aren't done after our children leave home or retire from our working jobs. We have been honing our life-skills for years. When we can connect our passions with our developed talents and skills, who knows what can happen? You can feel the energy and calling in your heart when these things unite. From my experience, when I allow the Universe to lead me and trust the process, the result is more amazing than I would have thought possible. That doesn't mean it is easy. I am challenged in ways I never thought I could handle—computer skills, writing skills, learning about publishing, marketing and much more. I can do this because I know this is where I need to be at this moment. Assisting myself, and others, to add meaning to our lives, and transcending the everyday grind that can bog us down, keeps me going. You too will find your place when you realize that there is one out there for you. No one else has your unique set of skills, gifts and talents. Unlocking them may take a few years. I beg you not to hide your light, but let it shine so that all of us will benefit from your contribution.

Farewell and Moving: Leaving with Intention

As you become aware of moments in your life that need tending, your parameters broaden to include more than you had previously considered. Instinctively most people know that job changes, moving, and leaving are ripe with opportunity for growth. By taking a hard look at each situation, you can then begin to understand what it is that you yearn for to mark this passage. Having the courage to ask for what you want can be one of life's hardest lessons, especially for women. Reading these stories will hopefully help you move into the place where you ask, take the risk of doing something out of your comfort zone, and trust that the process will help to open your heart to receive the support you desire as you move through change.

This is a process story. Sarah initiated the change herself. She chose to move out of an unsatisfactory job. We follow her course of embracing this change to see where it leads her.

Changing Jobs

Sarah decided that she needed to quit her job. She had worked for her company for ten years. The job itself was OK, but the situation wasn't very rewarding, nor did she feel as if she was a valued employee. She was afraid to quit, as she was the most consistent breadwinner of her family. Yet she knew on a deep level that she needed to terminate this position.

Sarah's clear intention was to quit her job. The part of exploring what would happen next was now the issue. She felt strong enough to tell her husband that it was his turn to be the primary income provider for a while, until she figured out a new path. She ultimately decided that she needed to take a few months off to have some free time to see what would turn up for her. When she explained to her husband what was happening, he was finally able to get a steadier job and fill in for her while she was in transition.

As Sarah lived with her sabbatical, her areas of passion and interest started to percolate. She realized she was interested in helping older folks. She started exploring what opportunities might evolve in this new field. She ultimately found a job that was much more satisfying and nurturing for her as an activities director at a senior center.

This seems like a simple and straightforward story on the surface. When we look at it closely, we can see Sarah consciously moving through the steps of the formula, which guided her during her job search. She identified the intention of terminating an unsatisfactory job. She then explored what would happen if she didn't work for a while. She let go of the outcome for the moment as she allowed the processing to unfold. In this instance, Sarah didn't ask for community assistance. She was able to articulate what she needed for herself and enlisted the aid of her husband. What emerged was time without work, to finish her old job emotionally and be in the moment to explore opportunities that would engage her talent. By allowing this space, she moved into an understanding of what she wanted to do. It then took some more time to look into the actual job opportunities.

Read about Sam, who designed an unusual celebration honoring his departure from the community and the people in it who were important to him.

A Banquet without Food

Sam had been living in our community for a couple of years. His passion about life and his interests connected him easily with local people. He collected an eclectic group of friends. He was a musician, screenwriter, computer expert, psychic, and father of seven children. When he and his family decided they needed to move, Sam planned a goodbye party for himself, to celebrate his time in this place and this stage of his life. It was his intention to invite twenty-three people who had been influential during his stay to a "Banquet of the Senses."

The place he chose to use for the meeting was a lovely spot deep in the woods—a magical place that needed to be rented for the evening, even though Sam had no extra money. The guests arrived at the designated time to be greeted by a bowl of rocks. If a person wanted Sam to do a psychic reading that evening, she was invited to take a rock. Chairs were set in a circle with each person's name on it. Sam and some of his friends presented a wonderful musical program. As he had been packing, Sam gathered a group of items from his personal collection of "Stuff" which he passed out to each attendee as a present—a little carving, a rock, a crystal, a plant. Each guest received a recycled, handpicked gift that came straight from Sam's heart, and one he didn't have to pack for the move. Neither food nor beverage was available.

At the end of the gathering, Sam set out a little can for donations to help defray the cost of the hall. When the owner saw this, she declined any payment. Being part of this unforgettable evening was enough for her.

My reaction to hearing about this happening was one of awe on many levels. I admired the fact that Sam had the courage to throw himself such a memorable gathering to celebrate his time in the community. He knew who was important to him on this part of his journey. He knew what he wanted to do and offered a carefully orchestrated plan executed with passion and panache. He was letting go of this community by honoring them and himself, and was ready to move on to new challenges. Sam left town with a flourish.

This simple little story illustrates a way to stay connected with a special person doing a special job. Variations of this theme can be used in many situations. Tuck this little idea into your back pocket for later use.

Letters to Go

Jill Wilson is an extraordinary woman in her eighties who still works full-time on behalf of the children of the world. Her field of interest and expertise is nutrition. Her mission is to help South American countries start lunch programs in the schools. It is a rather fundamental activity, because if these kids eat and are better able to learn, they may grow up to be politically active, and then who knows what might happen! During the holidays, Jill needed to go to Chile to plan a large conference. She was dragging her feet, even though she needed to do this. She would be gone for fifteen days.

I wanted to do something for her to let her know she wasn't alone as she proceeded with her passion. Whatever was planned needed to be small, as she was traveling internationally. I also wanted this something to last the duration of her trip.

I decided to write fifteen notes to her with a date on each one. Each day, she could open a card with a message in it to let her know she was being loved and supported while she was away. I then realized that the messages would be more interesting and powerful if fifteen different people wrote one. Before long, I talked to enough people willing and eager to participate. I put an envelope in our church office where folks could drop off their cards. I collected them and took them to Jill before she left on her trip. Those of us left behind had the fun of knowing that each day she would be reminded that she is the hands and heart of the work and not alone. She is doing a job the rest of us can't do. We sent our gratitude and encouragement for all that she is doing on behalf of the children of the world.

I am writing this story before Jill has returned. I can do this because when we know what we want to do, have a plan, execute the plan, the rest will be just right as we let go of the outcome. Our hearts are in the right place, and however the scenario unfolds, it is out of our control. There is no need for follow-up, as we have let go of judgment and expectation. We put our energy into the project for Jill, and that is that!

Many young unmarried couples today decide to live together. For Annie this was a serious matter. We have few ceremonial role models in these cases, so Annie needed to dig deeply into her creative self to figure out what she wanted from a gathering. Here is what she did.

Moving in with Your Boyfriend

At age twenty-eight, Annie was involved with Paul in her first significant relationship. After dating and deciding they were serious, the two of them made a decision to move in together. This was a big deal for Annie. She wanted to acknowledge this change for herself and have it witnessed by close friends.

After everything was moved out of her apartment, Annie asked several close friends to meet her there. The stark emptiness of the space made a powerful statement. Annie asked that her friends come to offer her support for her decision, and affirm her in taking on the new role of a partner in cohabitation. Gifts were not invited nor expected.

When the group met, Annie began her gathering by setting up a circle. Everyone sat on the floor, as there were no chairs. Annie asked for each person to say what came into her heart with regard to the changes in Annie's life. In the flow of the responses and affirmations, advice and stories unfolded. Many of the friends mentioned that this change would not alter the friendships that had already been established with Annie. She had a fear of losing her close buddies when she made the transition and changed her status from single to partnered.

The entire process did not take longer than an hour. Annie listened carefully as she internalized the wisdom that her friends were giving her. The friends, in turn, felt honored by being asked to witness this transition. They took the time seriously as they attempted to understand and uphold Annie.

When the circle was finished, there was no food or party. Each person moved on into her own life. There was a feeling that the essence of what needed to happen was respected. Extra trimmings were not necessary in this instance. The physical space was clean and ready to leave. The acknowledgment of Annie's emotional move was also clean and prepared. Her friends were able to offer encouragement, continuing friendship, affirmations, as well as cautions on the new journey. Annie left her old apartment ready to face the new challenges and opportunities.

This next scenario is not unusual—an older couple needs to move from their beloved home to a smaller place where they can receive regular help and care. Even though they know the move is necessary, that doesn't make it easy. In this story the process helps to create a smoother transition.

Moving to a Retirement Home

Marie and Lon needed to move away from their cherished beach home to a place that was more suitable for their current situation. Lon had fallen and broken his hip. Their home was full of stairs. They were in their early eighties. Making the decision to move was difficult. Brad, their son, wanted the move to go as smoothly as possible for them. That is what I call his intention. How he chose to implement it was wonderful way of creating meaningful moments. It doesn't mean that this was fun. It does mean that Brad took time, energy and used his expertise to assist his parents in the process of moving.

Brad is a marketing and advertising person. His job includes making presentations. He can pinpoint the important issues and put them into a presentable and understandable package. He used these skills to assist his parents through the process of looking at the need for moving, available options and the steps to be taken.

The project started with a Part 1 presentation. It was clearly written down in large print with not too much information on any one page—very clear and direct. Brad, his sister and his parents had a copy, so that all could be on the same page during this process. Communication was a key factor. Part I was called "An Overview of Housing/Care Options." It included their current housing situation, their short-term housing options, where they could be long-term, and the next steps. This took place in May. Later in the month, when Part I was addressed and there was more information in the equation, he introduced Part 2, "Long-term Housing." This included an updated health evaluation of Lon, and also looked at a new appropriate single level house for them (with pros and cons), and how to proceed with a possible purchase. Part 3, "More Options," came out in late May as more information was available. They all realized that the house in question was not going to work. They moved on to look at retirement/assisted living possibilities in the area where they decided they wanted to move—with pros and cons all clearly listed. Each phase included next steps at the end. By mid-June, Part 4, called "More Long-Term Housing Options," was prepared and presented. Included in the proposal to sell the beach house were lists of all contractors and work to be done (so the house would fetch its maximum value) and by whom, a timeline for the work, and some actual moving plans.

At the time I am writing this, it is still a work in progress. What is important here is that Brad, using his intention, personal skill, and taking the time, has turned an overwhelming situation into a more manageable one. Looking at the decisions and tasks in smaller pieces, with the options outlined, his parents were able to digest a piece at a time. They were then able to make better, more informed decisions. At a time when Marie was busy taking care of Lon, and Lon was busy taking care of himself, the process of moving looked overwhelming. Brad assisted them in making the necessary choices at a time when it wasn't easy for them to do it alone.

Retirement

The opportunity for change offers a chance to develop perspective. What may seem like a huge tragedy may turn out to be the best thing that could happen. Sometimes at the time you don't know. What you do have control over is your response to what happens. Of course, initial feelings, (fear, rage disappointment, excitement) rush to the surface giving notice that something monumental is taking place. Once you acknowledge these sensations, you can receive the messages they offer, then choose a course of action. It's in creating a plan that you have your choice, and can tweak the experience from one of dread to one of enjoyable possibility.

Some retirees receive the proverbial gold watch, when the last thing they wanted was to leave their job. Some might be excited and can't wait to move on. Creating a meaningful event to acknowledge a retirement can tax our resourcefulness, yet can open the possibility of new adventure when the door is closed with respect and intention.

This unusual retirement event grew from thinking about Mike and his influences on his students. I wanted to find a way where people could relate back to him that he had helped them along in their academic careers.

Letters for Mike

Mike was ready to retire after teaching high school science, math, graphic design and shop for thirty years in our local high school. He is a dedicated person and affected many students in positive ways. My intention was to find a way to acknowledge his contribution to our community. After thinking about it, I felt that what might touch Mike would be to hear from his students. Learning how big a difference he made in someone's life, after devoting his career to it, could be a fulfilling way to mark Mike's moment of moving on.

Finding the students without asking Mike was a bit of a challenge. His wife, Lindsay, and I went to the high school and looked through the last thirty years of yearbooks. Lindsay tried to remember students who might have been in his classes. After compiling a long list, I then needed to start to chase down these students. I wrote a letter explaining the plan. It turned out that I didn't need to use it, because as I was sleuthing out the addresses of the students, I talked to people who passed along the word. The chain effect worked. I said that Mike was retiring at the end of the year and encouraged his former students to write him a note about whatever they wanted to share. They could mail it directly to his home address, so he would receive the letters himself—no hoopla or public fanfare. Mike is not the kind of guy who would want a big show attached to his retirement.

After identifying the intention, I tried to move into Mike's space to connect with what might work to honor him. Because he is rather private person, yet so committed to his students, the idea of the letters seemed to be a way to acknowledge him. Students could thoughtfully spend a few minutes writing and reflecting about this man who was influential in their lives. Upon receiving the notes, Mike could spend time privately processing and remembering each of these students without being in the public eye. Hopefully he would receive confirmation that his time and effort were worth the anxiety and headaches that accompany the teaching profession. Recalling some wonderful moments and exceptional students would help him close the door on this chapter of his life and prepare him for a positive next stage.

Divorce: Moving Through Unplanned Change

Divorce is a nasty rite of passage. It includes a death of a relationship, the breaking up of a family, the loss of a dream, and fear of the future. In our culture, we don't know how to help our friends, or ourselves, deal with it.

If you have a friend going through a divorce, ask if you can support her in a special way. It may be that you set up a time, just the two of you, where you can offer your total and complete attention, showing up to listen and be present.

If you are the one going through the divorce, take the time to figure out what you need and ask for it. It could be a weekend away with good friends. It could be time alone to process what is happening in your life. Only you know, at a gut level, what it is that will help sustain you through this particular challenge.

You may need to look deeply into your grief and anger to discover what is needed for you to move on. Perhaps a celebration, when the final papers are signed, is in order. Maybe writing a letter to your former partner, and inviting friends to come over as you burn it, would help signify the end of the relationship. You may need a new hair-do or a game of golf with the guys. The power of being witnessed, when going through a big change, can be healing. You know you are not alone. Take courage. Your friends want to know how they can help you—help them help you.

Read about a couple of creative ways that people marked their divorce, and from this action, were able to start the process of moving on with their lives.

This example is unique, and possibly unusual, as the couple created a ceremony both of them attended. Not every divorced couple is on good enough terms to tolerate a joint gathering, but in this case it happened.

A Time to Cut the Ties

A friend told me about a gathering to honor a divorce. It might seem like an odd thing to do, yet healing may begin to take place when the act of terminating a marriage can be witnessed. In this story, the divorcing couple, April and Donovan, were able to meet with their joint friends to enact this symbolic cutting of the ties that bind.

Guests were invited who knew April and Donavan as a couple. April invited her sister and two women from her friends' circle. Donavan invited his dad, brother and a guy from his Monday night football group. Each person participating brought, or obtained there, a yard length of ribbon, cord or yarn. All stood in a circle and began to weave the strands together until they were all quite intertwined, yet still had two distinct ends. The couple then cut the ribbons. What was one, was now two. As participants took their piece of yarn, they were encouraged to affirm both April and Donovan in their status of being single—verbalizing support, prayers, advice and more.

It was important to keep the tone positive and supportive. Just because the marriage didn't work didn't necessarily mean that either party was in the wrong. The ceremony allowed both of them to move out of that charged relationship with the backing of friends and family. They were reminded of their unique talents and gifts, which remained and were still available to them, even if they were not married. This marriage was over, yet there was more ahead in life.

Marriage commonly starts out with a huge kick-off. The dissolving of the marriage usually gets ignored, swept under the carpet, bitterly pretending that it didn't happen. Normally divorce is a trauma for the couple involved. The possibility of having it acknowledged can benefit the health of the individuals.

The described ceremony will work for couples who stay connected in some way—through their children, through a long-standing shared history, through a desire to close this mutual chapter in order to move on with less emotional baggage, and who are willing to meet together with their families and friends to acknowledge the split. This isn't an easy thing to do, but can help close the time in a positive way, for the individuals involved, as well as their family and friends.

Here we have a story about a woman who stayed in her home after the divorce. The space was cluttered with unfinished business. Read about what she did to clear it.

House Clearing

This story about divorce creates an opportunity to clear out the emotional space of a home. When a major transition takes place, like a divorce, having the courage to acknowledge it can be the start of the healing process. There are times when one person of the couple will stay in the previously shared space. To imagine that life will go on in the same way, without the partner, seems unlikely. If the change is witnessed and acknowledged, there is increased possibility for the place to be less charged and more emotionally available for those who stay.

Rita had recently finished a separation that ended in divorce. She was staying in the house she previously shared with her ex-husband. She felt she needed a house blessing. She asked a priest friend to come over, along with a small group of trusted friends, to help her move through the house. Each invited person brought food for a later dinner.

The priest asked which element Rita associated with the house—water, air, earth or fire. After thinking it over, she chose water. Water needs to be free flowing and clear, not stagnant. Its color is blue and is associated with power—according to the many ancient traditions that have used the elements as healing tools for centuries. It is also connected with the third chakra (one of the seven energy centers of the body according to Indian medicine), which includes rela-tionship issues. Each element has particular properties. The priest felt that the characteristics from the water would help support Rita as she moved through this transition. As the group toured the house, going from room to room, Rita carried some water and a light, symbolic of helping her see her way clearly.

The first room visited was the kitchen. The group stayed there for an hour and a half as Rita told about the memories that flooded through her as she sat in this room: all those lunches she had prepared for her kids; the romantic dinners with candles and daring new recipes that she spent hours planning for her husband; the scratches on the counter that came from dropping the can of tomatoes; the serious conversa-

147

tions with her daughter about dating and boys. She was able to identify the emotions she felt at different times in this kitchen. The spirit of the family resided in this room, as most of the important conversations took place here. She described the expectations that she felt from cooking and eating and care-taking.

The group moved on. In one of the kids' bedrooms, she described feelings associated with watching her children sleep, outgrow their cribs, and establish themselves as individuals. The group was able to give her input on what they were seeing, hearing and feeling, which added dimension and understanding to the process. The gathering started at ten in the morning and kept going until dinnertime. Rita was given a safe space to unlock and process the memories, experiences and emotions of this house, when her original family lived there. She was witnessed as she cleared the space of old vibrations. It was a house cleaning in an emotional sense. Rita was invited to clear out the space for new opportunities to move in. She didn't have to ignore or stuff away what had happened here. Speaking out loud, and having others hear her, diffused the power of the old experiences. The house was being made ready and available for whatever new was being offered to Rita.

This woman was having a hard time letting go of her marriage. Anger and grief kept her bound in an unhealthy way. When she finally realized what was going on, she asked some friends to help her through this stuck-ed-ness and this is what happened.

Sally's Wedding Dress

Sally was divorced six years ago. Since that time, she moved through life acting as if all was well with the world. Fortunately, she had a group of women friends who could see that this wasn't the case. She hadn't processed her loss and was still carrying a lot of hurt. Sally was able to see that by acknowledging her divorce with the support of her friends, she might be able to move on with a freer spirit. With help, Sally designed a symbolically irreverent, significant event, which hopefully would assist her in moving beyond her divorce.

Sally's friends witnessed as she dug a hole in her back yard. Into it she very carefully placed her wedding dress. She then proceeded to dump shovel loads of dirt onto this beautiful garment. As she dumped the dirt, she was able to release some of her long held dreams and hopes. She was letting go of the last remnants of her lost marriage. She realized how much she had been clinging to the past when the rest of the world was moving on. She was symbolically burying her marriage and finally letting it go. Having her friends surround her, uphold her and witness this act of release helped Sally move through a difficult process. At the end, all were laughing

149

when they thought of someone in the future digging in the yard and finding the remains of a wedding dress. What would an anthropologist think of this?

Hopefully theses stories will help you think of how you might free your own spirit to begin healing from a traumatic or grief-filled experience. It is a tough chore to tackle, yet the brave person reaps the benefits of freedom from the weight of the unnecessary emotional baggage. When you set your intention, you may not want to embark upon this project alone. Be sure to ask your friends for help. Sometimes several minds working together on a problem or task can create lots of laughter, or tears, while facing a difficult experience.

New Roles: Taking on a New Function and Responsibility

Taking on a new role means modifying behavior, function and activities that are expected. When you become aware of the many times you choose change, or change is thrust on you, you'll be in a position to transform events into opportunities. Many of the adjustments you don't ask for. Inviting support and help as you move toward a path of understanding and acceptance may propel you down the road when you feel stuck. When you consciously think about what can happen with the shift, you will understand that marking the moment may help everyone involved appreciate the new role, and respond with grace and awareness.

Our stories identify several examples of change in people's lives and what was done to honor them. Becoming a mother-in-law is an unusual theme for a celebration. You will be amazed at the depth of sharing that surfaced from taking the time to look at this topic. A woman realizes she hasn't fully accepted and processed the role of being a widow, so invites family to witness her passage. Accepting a new sister-in-law into the family opens hearts for a sincere welcome. A woman bravely accepts the responsibility of becoming an elder. A mother valiantly connects with her son in prison, helping him find a place to value himself. Enjoy these stories of boldness.

How many mother-in-law celebrations have you attended? You will be amazed at what happened in the following unusual situation and celebration.

Becoming a Mother-in-Law

MOTHER-IN-LAW

Becoming a mother-in-law is one of life's unsung transitions that could be lovely to celebrate. The addition of a daughter or son-in-law shifts family dynamics forever. Some women may wish to move into this new role with the conscious support and backing of their friends. This story is about Laura, who wanted to acknowledge and explore this new role in her life.

Laura has one son. One day he announced that he was planning to marry a young woman not of his family's faith, and quite a bit younger. Laura began to realize that her dreams for her son didn't necessarily follow this particular scenario. She had work to do to address and resolve these issues of her dreams and his. It had less to do with the new bride herself than Laura working through the changes that were taking place in her own family. She bravely tackled her emotional responses. How would it work when the new person didn't share the same faith background? How could she rearrange her dreams to support this new relationship? How could she reinvent the role of mother-in-law to embrace the new bride and feel an honest connection with her?

The wedding took place in the Summer and was a lovely occasion. By then, Laura had become more acquainted with her son's fiancée, and began to appreciate her as a person in her own right. The two women enjoyed working on the wedding together and were beginning to establish a friendship.

In the Fall, after the wedding, Laura expressed to a friend that many of her close women friends hadn't been a part of the wedding. She felt that a part of her, in her new role as mother-in-law, was missing from the interactions she had with these women. One friend volunteered to host a "Welcome to Mother-in-Law-hood" party for Laura, so that she could be acknowledged in this new role. This party was moving into new territory for most of the guests, as none had been part of such an occasion. Most thought it was an interesting idea and were glad to be a part of this witnessing for Laura, if that was what she wanted.

As the evening approached, a potluck dinner with an Asian theme was planned. Fifteen women accepted invitations, including the new daughter-in-law and the young woman who was her maid of honor at the wedding. The others were mostly in Laura's age range. All but two women had mothers-in-law. Three were already mothers-in-law themselves.

On the evening of the party, they enjoyed a festive dinner of delicious food and conversation. Afterwards all gathered in a circle in the living room. The party was near Halloween and the facilitator came in dressed as a witch. She talked about the stereotypical view of the mother-in-law that includes derogatory jokes. Suddenly the facilitator yanked off her hat and black cloak. Underneath was a dazzling, elegant, jewel-bedecked outfit. The women saw the transformation of the role of the mother-in-law. Witnessing this change was a fun and graphic way for all to relate to embracing a new role model that can be created by any individual.

As the evening proceeded each woman introduced herself and explained how she knew Laura. The invitation had asked for stories, jokes or advice about being a mother-in-law. The guests were asked to set a sacred circle—one in which respect and confidentiality were honored, judgment was left out and attentive listening was agreed upon. The woman acting as facilitator then asked the question of the group "What drives you nuts about your mother-in-law? What do you appreciate about her?" A magic wand was used for a talking stick to pass around to define the speaker. Many women had never taken the time to think much about the position of mothers-in-law in their lives. These women are role models as the next generation moves into that same situation themselves. The stories that emerged about these interesting mothers-in-law were funny, heart-breaking, sometimes full of grief, admiration or gratitude. One guest realized that she never really had a mother-in-law as the woman was an alcoholic and not emotionally available. Another grieved because her mother-in-law had died before she was married. She felt she had missed out on a significant relationship. One woman joyfully exclaimed that she had the best mother-in-law ever, as the mother-in-law supported the family with babysitting, emotional support, meals and good humor. Amidst the tears, laughter and awe, all realized that this gathering was for everyone, not just Laura. Together they explored a part of their hearts and lives that hadn't been touched. Because Laura set forth to acknowledge her own transition, she allowed the group to process their own experiences in ways that will assist them on their personal journey of becoming mothers-in-law, or appreciating their own mothers-in-law in a new way.

The evening ended with each guest being given a small card with an envelope. They were then asked to write about a characteristic of Laura's that they felt would uphold her in her new role. These were then given to her to read at her leisure. In this way, she had something concrete to save and remind her of her positive attributes, as well as the memory of the evening.

Even though this was an unusual topic for a gathering, those present felt honored to take the time to reflect upon this sometimes revered, sometimes mocked, role of mother-in-law. Being invited to share stories deepened awareness about the role this woman plays in our lives. Whether a guest was already a mother-in-law, or she thought about her own mother-in-law, the perspective was rich, rewarding and enlightening. Laura's inspiration to offer the gathering benefitted all.

Read about a widow who spent some time soul-searching after losing her husband. She was alone, but needed and wanted a few close women to help her acknowledge her passage from widow to single woman. She was ready to let go of parts of her life that were no longer relevant. This woman shows valuable insight as she moves into the rest of her life.

Widow's Passage

Ellie's husband had been dead for five years. Their marriage had been long and happy. She loved her husband. She appreciated the companionship and stability that he had offered. The couple produced three daughters. Ellie also had a niece who was especially close to her.

Ellie called the four young women and invited them to go with her to Hawaii for a vacation. The girls knew that something was up, but didn't know what was happening, as a trip of this kind was unusual for their family. They stayed in a lovely beachfront hotel on Maui. They ate, explored, hiked and did all the usual fun, tourist activities. One afternoon, Ellie asked them to meet at the water's edge. She carried several pieces of paper. She told the girls that they were in Hawaii because her husband had hated the place and never wanted to visit there. She loved to travel, but he traveled so much with his work that he always wanted to stay home when vacation time came. Ellie waded into the water and read from her papers. "I let go of. . . ."

The girls had been asked to witness the process of Ellie letting go of old habits and behaviors that came with her life of living with her husband. She read the paper, then tore it into tiny shreds and tossed it into the sea. She had no distaste, anger, or remorse for her old life. She wanted to let go of the parts that would no longer serve her as she embraced a new life alone.

The girls found the process empowering, watching their mother and aunt consciously turning a corner on her life. Ellie was remaking herself in a positive way. She asked those women closest to her to stand with her as she stated her intentions aloud, and got rid of what was not working. She came to the event with a clear conscience, and she returned to her home with a clear perception of where she wanted to go next, and how she wanted to be in the world for her remaining years. It had taken her several years to process the loss, grief and changes at the death of her husband. The idea of emerging as a new and different human being had been percolating in her brain for some time. She had no models for what she wanted to do. She looked deep into her heart for guidance and came up with this plan that worked for her.

Ellie went on with her life and did extensive traveling. When I heard this story in a group setting, one woman commented that Ellie must have been in great health at her age to make these changes and commitments for herself. Her niece, who was telling this story, remarked that Ellie was a very frail person in her body, but her spirit was so strong that she was able to do what she set out to do in spite of her health.

Marty's son, Peter, was nineteen when he was sent to prison for twenty years for his involvement in a drug-related crime. You can imagine the ongoing angst in that family. Yet through all the turmoil and despair, Marty decided to focus on what she could do for Peter, rather than get lost in pity, victimization or anger. Hers is a story of creativity and courage, giving support to her son while he is doing his prison time.

Prison Art

Many inmates finish their sentences and get out of jail without resources to uphold them in finding jobs, a place to live, or start-up money. Over-crowding, limited job and educational opportunities inside the system, leave little room for hope. Marty's intention was clear—to come up with some sort of plan to help Peter feel motivated and secure—to help prepare him for his reentry into society.

Peter had always been a great artist. From a young age, he doodled and drew extraordinary pictures. During his adolescent years, he specialized in exceptional graffiti masterpieces located on walls, freeways, tunnels and freight trains. His West Coast underground reputation was well established. Trains, in particular, were his specialty.

Marty felt that the connection for Peter from prison to the outside could be his art. He constantly sketched on the letters he sent home to family and friends. These drawings became treasures for those who received them. Perhaps Marty could to find a way validate this talent, which would give him an outlet for his creative self, rebuild his self esteem, and maybe lead to a source of income to prepare him for living in the outside world.

Art supplies were ordered from catalogues with money he earned from being an electronics technician. His family sent him what materials were allowed. He needed to be careful with his supplies, as they were limited. He chose acrylics as his medium.

Over time, Peter sent pictures home. Marty framed them and put them up in their home and at their restaurant, where friends and customers asked to buy

them. Marty couldn't bear to part with the originals, so she found a business that does a special process to make them into posters. These she would sell, make some profit for Peter, and advertise the message that there is locked up talent in our prison system that needs to be seen. Here was the beginning of a small business enterprise that Marty could set up and run for Peter until he could do it himself.

Marty created a website where she could sell the posters. She hopes to represent other "in house" artists on this site and sell their work. Their art offers an avenue for expressing the inexpressible where it can be shared, thus perhaps creating greater understanding and compassion for the incarcerated and their talents.

Marty is still bogged down with the legalities and logistics of what she can and cannot do with regard to the prison system. Is it legal to sell art pieces on the outside and put the money away for her son for a later time? Can she represent more artists than her son? How would all this affect the other prisoners inside the jail? Many details are still to be worked out, but Marty feels called to act as their agent. The mission was initially for her son, and now it has turned into supporting other inmates as well. Her plan is still unfolding as the project takes more shape and definition. Yet Marty knows that she is committed to assist these men who have made grave mistakes and to help them to connect with their talents and passion so they can move into the realm of personal expression. What inspiring goals sprang forth from a simple intention of helping her son to develop some coping skills for his future.

     This unusual story marks the moment by devising a plan of support for Peter. The project is ongoing until his release, yet these moments in prison, where Peter can create, have an outlet for his emotions through his art and make a place for himself, are significant. Marty intentionally searched out a strategy that would work for their unique situation. After exploring options and revisiting Peter's strengths, she knew deep down that art would be the channel for him. She has more work to do with this undertaking as she follows her heart. In the end, she is letting go of any preconceived notion of what should happen and trusts that the project is unfolding in the way that it needs. The men and women in our prison system can teach us, and bring forth gifts, when they are stripped of all outside distractions. They get to "draw" from inside and Marty is offering the gift sharing their art on the online gallery soon to come.

     Honoring a new sister-in-law is almost in the bridal shower category, but as you read this story you will feel the distinction. These women truly make the decision to invite the new bride into their close circle, as she will be an intimate part of their family. The sisters want her to know that she is accepted into the already existing group and they are ready to share their lives with her.

A New Sister

Four sisters decided to welcome a new sister into the family. This close-knit group realized they wanted to do something special for Janice to show their love and acceptance of her. They explored ideas and asked Janice what she might want. Many ideas were offered: a bachelorette party, going to a nursery and picking out a plant, each guest making a beaded bracelet that Janice could wear, writing an appreciation letter to her on decorated paper, planning a traditional shower. Finally, they came up with the following plan and put it into action.

A lovely enclosed porch adjoined the big redwood house. Flowers and living greens of all varieties circled the entire space except for two doors. A Buddha rested solidly in one corner with a graceful gold pendant added to his head. The ceiling held several wrought iron candleholders. Looking out between the flowers, one could see the distant lower garden. White wicker table and chairs added welcoming warmth to the room. In the late afternoon, after darkness fell, a group of four sisters-in-law and one teenage daughter began to prepare the space for a welcoming ceremony for their new sister/mother to be. As many candles as the women could find replaced electric lights lending an otherworldly quality to the space. The young woman selected soft ceremonial Celtic music. The air temperature offered by nature was perfect. The scent of the fragrant flowers gently tickled the nose. The scene was set. The new sister entered the almost mystical room wearing her wedding dress. She sat on a stool in the middle of the room and closed her eyes. A small bell announced the opening of the ceremony. One sister quietly reminded the women that they were gathered to welcome Janice into the family. As a group, they decided to offer "an angel wash" to enfold her with tender touch. The angel wash is a magical expression of love. The gentle, silent stroking with hands is done with specific meaning. In this case, a welcome to the family and blessings on the new role of wife were the messages conveyed through the silence and soft contact. The women proceeded in silence to stroke Janice gently with their hands until each person felt they were done. The room vibrated with loving energy.

When the angel wash was finished, one sister asked each member of the group to think of a word or short phrase that spoke to their experience. One woman collected them all, and then read them aloud so all could enjoy and appreciate what they had experienced together. These little words and phrases molded themselves into a group poem that Janice could keep as a reminder of her exquisite experience. A few minutes bonded the women in a special way that none will forget and started their journey as family.

This is my personal story. It could go in the menopause chapter, but I prefer it here in new roles, as the goal was to embrace a new self more than focus on the physical body. The celebration was a long time in coming, but finally materialized. The intention was clear, yet the implementation was blurry for a while. I trusted that when the time was right, it would blossom. And that's what happened.

Sparkling Seasoned Woman

Long about the time my body was entering the menopause corridor, I became aware of the importance of the physical changes to come. The emotional and spiritual shifts taking place simultaneously caused this already unstable machine to teeter precariously. My body was letting me know, in a huge way, that life would never be the same. Yet in a larger picture, what did all this mean? Who was going to emerge from these changes? Should I slide in to old age, or could I claim my place? I decided to embrace my next role and persona. The process took several years to unravel into a presentable package.

Once I determined the intention of claiming myself as an elder, I needed to decide if I could do this for myself. I am used to being in front of groups because I am a teacher, but to plan a gathering and have it all about me was a challenge. I finally realized I was called to do this. I needed to be a role model for aging gracefully. I had to get out of my own way and tackle this intense and life changing issue.

I moved into the exploration phase of the project—asking myself questions about me. Since I was choosing to be proactive, who do I want to become? What is my vision of myself? What kind of power can older women wield if we take ourselves seriously? Images of wisdom, crone, wrinkles, and rocking on the front porch took on new significance. Yet I realized I can create my own reality.

After several years of tossing around thoughts, fears, and ideas, the vision of me became clearer, and I wanted to name it. The words "woman" and "sparkle" resonated. I love to sparkle, but I wanted more. What was the other little piece? While on a trip to Tucson, I noticed a clothing store called the Seasoned Woman. The image jumped out at me, and I knew I wanted to be a Sparkling Seasoned Woman for the rest of my life. From this point on, I could move into the planning stage of claiming my new role.

I thought carefully about who I wanted to surround me during this crossing. I needed support and didn't want to have to explain why I was doing this. I wanted women who understood ritual and felt ready to witness this process. My daughters drove in from Portland. Most of the rest of the guests had participated in my classes, and some were long-time friends who shared a similar spiritual mindset.

I hadn't planned on food, but friends suggested that we needed to honor the ancient tradition of women and food. I compromised with offering chocolate dipped strawberries and champagne.

Even the planning stage took a couple of years. By the time the celebration was ready, I was ready. It was my sixtieth year.

Here's how the day unfolded:

We met at my home, which is located on the cliff with a view of the sea. The day in May was lovely with sun bathing the huge tree trunks outside the window. The long-stemmed flowers brought by each woman were placed in large vases until we needed them later. We gathered in the living room—twenty-five women, dressed in finery, ready to birth ourselves again.

In the opening circle, each woman introduced herself and explained how we were acquainted. I am constantly amazed at the richness that this small ritual brings—little stories, appreciations, connections and laughter already permeated the room, and we were just beginning.

After the first round, we moved into the second circle of verbal offerings that addressed the passage. Readings, books, songs, stories filled the room from the deep well of women's wisdom. These women had taken to heart the idea of crossing over the line to claim the role of elder. Whether they were already "of an age," or knew that they would eventually reach this stage, all were deeply involved in considering what this meant. They were supporting me in my statement and coming out, and at the same time, they were honoring themselves.

We have a room in our house large enough to put up a ping-pong table, which I set up with stations of paper plates filled with beads, feathers and doodads. Each

Celebration of the

Sparkling Seasoned Woman

Please join me, Paula Pugh, as I celebrate claiming the rest of my life.

Intention: Share with friends the passage of moving past menopause and into the world as I claim it now.

Place: My home at 91 Brackenwood Avenue, Langley, WA
Date: Saturday, May 21, 2005
Time: From 3-5ish in the afternoon
What: We shall make some fringes to add to a shawl. If you have small beads or tokens to add to supplies already on hand, please feel free to bring them. Color theme is silver, purple, gold and black. If you have poems, music, jokes, advice, photos, stories, etc. to share that will support all women as we make this passage please bring them. (totally optional)
Bring: A single long stemmed flower
Attire: Fun, frivolous, festive, flighty and feisty

RSVP: 360-221-5423

167

woman was given a needle and golden thread on which to make a piece of fringe that would then be attached to the translucent black garment I was wearing. This didn't seem like it would be such a big deal, but the process of making a little fringe was a bit more arduous than expected. The time spent working with our hands, creating and chatting, made a timeless camaraderie and permeated the space as we explored our deepest hearts through working with our fingers. Eventually, everyone finished her project. I immediately pinned many of them onto my gauzy cover, so I could wear them for the rest of the day.

We gathered up our flowers and moved outside under the huge fir tree that houses our eagle nest and protects our home. We made a flower arch, just like the military does with their swords for special occasions. I began the journey and moved through the smell of the flowers and the supportive, cradling energy of these women. I walked slowly toward the water and took my place at the end of the flower arch, and the others followed. The physical movement of passing through the flower portal moved me to tears at the same time as filling me with the courage to move ahead with conviction, love and purpose.

We returned to the inside of the house to celebrate with strawberries and champagne.

I moved into my role of being old enough to be a grandma, of not fighting the wrinkles and sags, of observing with awe the wisdom that so many years on the planet can grant us. I established my being. I claimed my identity. I asked for what I needed and wanted, and I accepted the support of my friends for this crossing. The ritual allowed me to take myself seriously and affirm this course. It was a big deal for me. The lessons learned about myself were rich. I am standing stronger on my path now that it is acknowledged. I can honestly recognize that I have crossed the line into being a person entering the "wise elder" part of my life. I couldn't have done it alone. This is no end but a beginning. The excitement of whatever is coming next leaves me glowing with anticipation. Watch out—here comes the Sparkling Seasoned Woman!

This is a most unusual story on many levels. It is political. I heard it on the radio. It was open to any Canadian who wanted to participate. I applaud this radio station for being innovative and inclusive, celebrating a change of government—amazing!

A New President

I was blown away one morning in January 2009 as I listened to our radio station. CBC-2, which we receive because we live close to the Canadian border, was transmitting a special program to welcome our new President-to-be Obama called "49 Songs North of the 49th Parallel." From January 5-16th, CBC invited Canadians to help select the top songs that would best define Canada to the new President. The project was an instant success as people felt excited with a means of expressing their joy with the change of government in the U.S. Songs like:

"Affairs of the Heart": Marjan Mozetich
"Both Sides Now": Joni Mitchell
"Hymn to Freedom": Oscar Peterson Trio
"Rise Up": Parachute Club
"Mon Pays": Gilles Vigneault

A radio stationed devised a way to recognize this moment in history allowing citizens to participate and to show President Obama that they cared about the political changes taking place. Meaningful moments can come in diverse packages. Keep your eyes and ears open. You may be surprised at what you notice!

Coming of Age: Growing Up

Planned coming of age events are not common in today's American society. Unplanned experiences seem to replace what could be a lovely acknowledgment of moving from child to adult, or woman to elder. Kids make their own rituals because there isn't anything else to define this shift: drugs and sex come to mind to fill the void. Other cultures pay tribute to these passages better than we do. We may need to look into traditions from other lands as we struggle to invent an observance that will work for us.

We have several examples of people stepping out and searching for ways to add meaning to these transitions. After reading these, maybe you too will be inspired to figure out something for your young friends and maturing adults.

Our first example tells of a book that explains ancient times when rites of passage were in place and what they meant to the girls and the community. We can learn from these stories of old.

Transition from Girl into Woman

Many cultures honor the passage from girlhood to womanhood—a time when a young woman moves through puberty, when her body is developing from the shape of a child to that of a woman. There are not too many transitions in life that are more monumental than this one for women. Our culture, unfortunately, is not one that seems to have developed traditions, meaningful moments or even much helpful dialogue to move smoothly through this time. In fact, our patriarchal culture has put a negative cast on this most natural and wonderful passages. Menstruation is often referred to as the "curse"—not much honoring in that comment. Being part of a patriarchal society means that we as women need to create value to our womanhood. We are not like men. We have unique gifts, which include the wonder of the ultimate creation of child-bearing. Today women are encouraged to pretend that they don't have a period. Our role models show us how to plow through life as a man without connecting to the rhythms of our body's language. It is not just the job of women to honor girls. Men also need to acknowledge to their daughters. We will look at some opportunities to do that in this section of the book.

In the book by Anita Diamant called *The Red Tent* (St. Martin's Press, 1997), young females look forward to their bleeding time, as this is when they will be accepted into the red tent and into the mysteries of being a woman. At this time, there is an initiation and the older women take the time to teach the new inductee what they will need to know to be a wife, lover, mother, grandmother, cook and all the roles necessary for women in that culture.

Some Native American traditions have a women's sweat lodge. This also honors the passage for a young woman and she is allowed to participate in the sweat lodge when it is her time of the month. Women retreat in their bleeding time to respect what their bodies are telling them. During this segregated period, the girls are also taught what they will need to be women of the tribe.

In our culture, we need to invent an honoring so that girls do not need to have sex as their own way of creating a rite of passage. We need to affirm them so they will honor their bodies, understand the gift they have of creation within them, and the special feminine wisdom available to them. Many of us—girls and boys—don't want to leave the safety of childhood. It is scary to think of becoming an adult. As grown-ups, we can assist in this transition time by acknowledging the changes that are happening. We can help our youth in developing the tools necessary for their adult lives. Fortunately or unfortunately, the best teaching is role modeling. That is also the most difficult task for any of us—to walk our talk. So staying on track personally and working with our youth can have a huge affect on their desire to be caring, stable, healthy adults.

The first story tells of creating a ritual and taking the time to visit with the young women important in one's life. Working with our hands and talking are what women do well. I used these basic concepts when planning this celebration.

Making Wisdom Dolls

I am fortunate to have several wonderful nieces for whom I wanted to acknowledge their passage into puberty. What has developed is a mini-honoring of their coming of age. When the girl is about twelve or thirteen, she comes over to the island to spend a day with me. I have a little doll kit that we make together. In the time-honored tradition of women working with their hands, we create, with fabric, feathers, yarn and pipe cleaners, a reminder of this day. This little doll has quite a personality. She symbolizes the access the girls have to their own inner wisdom and guidance, which is available to them through life. As we work with our hands, I talk about some things that I wished I had known when I was their age, the cycles of our women's bodies.

- How women cycle each twenty-eight days, which happens to be the same time frame as the moon cycles the earth, as the tides rise and fall. If a woman is very in tune with nature, she will cycle in harmony with the moon.
- How women can be so in tune with each other that they can begin to cycle together as their bodies conform to a strong female leader in the group. Girls find this can happen in a dorm setting or even in the workplace, if there are many women.
- How our own internal cycle has a flow of outgoing creative time before ovulation, and an inward reflective time, as we move into our bleeding time

My hope is that by hearing about how amazing their body is and the messages that spring forth from it, that they will be able to honor their womanhood and femininity. This will assist them in making rational decisions at later points in their lives. At the very least, each niece and I have had fun. Sometimes the girls just listen. Sometimes they have made insightful comments followed with discussion. I try to stay open to the outcome and let them have some say in what direction the conversation will go.

After this more intense time, we walk downtown, have an ice cream cone and enjoy the beauty of being outside.

This isn't an earthshaking moment, yet hopefully I am helping them appreciate themselves. I am acknowledging a significant time in their lives, taking the time to affirm them as emerging women, and hopefully keeping open a door for further discussion if needed. I cherish the time we have together. It is probably more special for me as Auntie than for them as the growing up girls.

We now have a story of a young man and his adult friends who offer to help him design his own passage of recognition. Allowing Thomas to take part in the plans also helps diffuse the discomfort that might arise from trying something new and gets him enthused about the event.

Thomas Designs his Passage to Manhood

Thomas was thirteen years old. The men closest to him in his life decided they wanted to do something special for him to help him realize that he wasn't alone as his body changed and his role in life became more complex. Thomas' dad and several other men asked Thomas to join them in designing an occasion that would be meaningful for him. The adults themselves didn't have much role modeling in this area. Including Thomas in the process helped turn the adventure into something that would work for all of them.

Thomas decided he wanted to go camping. He also gave the names of several other guys he would like to have included on the trip. The men, young and older, planned the excursion and off they went into the mountains. They hiked in and set up camp. They explored the area and set up a campfire in the evenings. It was during evenings when the men would share their stories of growing up—of the pain, the fear, the awkwardness, as well as some times of fun. The men made a place where these stories of growing up could be heard and shared. Thomas would know that he wasn't alone on this journey of discovery. He also realized that he had a network of caring men who would be available to support him when he might have questions as he went through his teen years and beyond.

A mom has a brilliant idea to help her son define who he is by saving important treasures. A record of his life emerged through this process and he could follow his own development.

Life Box

When her son was seven or eight, Ellen started a Life Box, a simple way for him to save things that had meaning. She spotted a big, blue, lidded box sprinkled with moons and stars at Nordstrom's Rack (about 10" x 14" x 8') and scooped it up. It was the perfect next step after a baby book. She put into it all the drawings, awards, special schoolwork, and newspaper clippings she'd been saving in a messy pile and presented Billy with this Life Box on his birthday. She explained that it was for storage for things he wanted to save for the future—that it would eventually contain some of the story of his life.

Billy loved the idea, and soon the box was full of ribbons from the County Fair, drawings of Greek soldiers,  programs from plays, and favorite photos. He tucked in his favorite t-shirt. When he outgrew the pink shell he used as a talisman to fall asleep, it went into the box. Some of the medals earned by his grandfather during World War II went into the box, too, as Billy became fascinated with military history. He put in old diaries and the travel journal he kept while bouncing around Central America with his parents on local buses. Though she continued to tear out newspaper clippings and save programs for the Life Box, it was clearly Billy's project now.

Eventually, she had to buy a second Life Box, and by the time he graduated from college, both boxes were full to the brim. When he came home to sort through his "stuff" to move to his first apartment, he spent a whole afternoon looking through the treasures in his Life Box and thinking about his story so far. He asked his parents to hold the boxes for him until he had his own house, being unwilling to drag them from apartment to apartment and risk their loss. Last week, Ellen managed to sneak in an invitation to his wedding and a copy of the engagement photos into the Box. This would be a fitting close to his childhood and adolescence. Ellen said she wouldn't be surprised if some time down the line Billy and his fiancée start Life Boxes for their own children after the baby books are full.

This interesting story centers on older women who never had a coming of age celebration when they were young, and decided they wanted one even if they were past thirteen. This is what they did.

Revisiting Girlhood

I facilitate retreats for women on the subject of health issues, especially connecting the Mind/Body/Spirit. I love these retreats as I have quality time to meet incredible women who are willing to look at their lives in a new way. The retreats have a format. There are four sessions and each session has a topic. In one of my retreats, I was planning on addressing issues of nutrition and exercise for the third session. After we finished the second session, I knew that this particular group was too knowledgeable about those topics for me to add much. So instead of panicking, I asked them what they might like to do for our third session. We had just finished a time focused on menstruation and menopause. We talked about transitions in women's lives—from child to maiden to crone. These women ranged in age from twenty-four to seventy-four. None of them had been honored with a transition ceremony when they were going through puberty. What these women decided to do was create a rite of passage for themselves—to move from girlhood to womanhood. It was as if there was a hole in their lives that needed filling, and it wasn't too late.

What these women created for themselves was profound. For me, knowing when to let go was a critical piece and not easy for a facilitator. I was able to honor the creative spirit and let these women use their personal gifts to honor themselves as women, when others in their lives had not done it. We witnessed for each other and welcomed the forgotten girl to the honored position of womanhood.

The retreat center had a basket of large, colored chiffon scarves. Each woman picked a scarf, focusing on the color that spoke to her. We danced with the scarves, making flowing patterns. We each found a song to sing, or a CD and I played my violin, all reaching to discover an expression of what this passage meant. We were able to find a massage table as all of the women wanted to feel the hands of the others on them in a soft and supportive way. While "their" music played, the woman was covered with her scarf and gently massaged and stroked by the others. Emotionally each person had her own experience. Afterwards we gathered in a circle and shared what this meant.

I loved the experience of a retroactive coming of age ceremony, and relished the fact that I hadn't "planned" it in our retreat time. We created our own meaningful moment. The element of surprise added wonder to the occasion.

What is important to know is that you can make this transition at any time. It isn't too late to gather a like-minded group to design your own passage—perhaps in conjunction with your own daughter's passage. Open your hearts to possibility and let it flow into your life.

Menopause: Crossing into Mid-Life

Menopause is a transition for older women whose lives will never be the same. Gone are the childbearing years. What comes next?

Since men and women are living longer lives, we have many years of productive time ahead. The average life expectancy in 1900 was forty-nine. Today it is well into the eighties. How we choose to use this time is up to us. Since the extra years are a relatively new phenomena, we are called to invent a new way of being—embracing the time as elders. We must decide what we can do to unlock our elder magic and have an effect on the world. I have several friends who have signed up for the Peace Corps, and they are senior citizens.

Read about how a few women have processed this change to open themselves for a new direction.

From looking inward, the woman in this story courageously set a space for reexamining her own experience of menopause and sharing that experience with others. She wasn't sure what would happen, but was willing to put it out there and let it be. She was in touch with her intuitive guidance, which didn't let her down.

Simple Acknowledgment of Menopause

Barbara had reached menopause. She didn't want to let this passage go unnoticed. She had no role models to acknowledge this significant passage, so she invented an occasion that worked for her.

Barbara has a seven-year-old son who attends a local private school. Most of the moms who have seven-year-olds are younger than Barbara. That fact didn't slow her down, as she felt that these were the women in her life who could support her in celebrating this change of life.

The school children were going on a camp-out, and many of the moms were acting as chaperones. While on this school outing, Barbara asked the women to join her in a gathering when the children were otherwise occupied. The women met together and Barbara told them that she was going into menopause. She mentioned her feelings about what was happening to her: her dreams, her reservations, and the changes going on in her body. She then opened the circle for others to speak. Some women talked about their own daughters and dreams of creating transitions for them. Some talked about their own experiences with their bodies and their relationships to their cycles. Barbara noticed that whatever was said by each woman was offered in a respectful and sacred way. Toward the end of the evening, one of the moms, who also happened to be an artist, got up and started a spontaneous dance in which all the moms participated. Deep connection had been established when Barbara had the courage to recognize her need for being with a group of women during this transition time. She convened a space to be heard and hear others. When the gathering was over she felt loved, witnessed and ready to move forward into the next part of her personal unfolding.

The next example isn't so much a story as a reflection on the menopause experience and an explanation of perhaps why it isn't often acknowledged. As we read about what some women have done to celebrate the change, we finally have some models.

Illusive Menopause

One reason why you may not see so many menopause rituals is that the process can take as long as ten years. Many women don't realize this. They think that there is a specific time when it starts and moment in time when you are done. That isn't the case. You can slip and slide into perimenopause, dip into the depths of full-blown menopause and trickle out the other side over a period of years, unless surgically induced—as in a hysterectomy.

The rule of thumb for being finished with menopause is being without a period for a full year. A woman may go nine months without one, have one, and then have to start counting all over again. If you are not interested in being pregnant, then you need to be careful until you are sure that you are done with your fertile time.

Since the duration of the passage is so long, it is hard to pinpoint just when you might want to celebrate, and then exactly what is it you want to do? If you realize the longevity of the process and are willing to embrace the many gifts it has to offer, you will come up with the perfect intention for yourself. Our recipe is ideal for this sort of nebulous experience as it helps pinpoint what exactly it is that you want to acknowledge.

Mary did her homework about menopause. She talked to friends and professionals about what could happen to her emotionally and physically during this time. Read how she decided to honor herself in order to move through the unsettling experience with grace.

Meno-Pause

When Mary was in her early forties, she started noticing some changes in her body and temperament. She had a short fuse. She would suddenly fling off her clothes. Her sleep patterns shifted and she wasn't sleeping well. All this was a formula for disaster in her private life as well as at work. Even though she didn't know much about menopause, she instinctively felt that perhaps this had something to do with the changes. How was she going to handle all this? She wanted to keep her relationships with her children, husband and her co-workers. What could she do?

Mary realized that educating herself was probably the best line of defense, so she moved into research mode. As she explored this topic, she found many interesting interpretations about what was happening and how to handle the symptoms. She looked into the common medical practices of giving hormone therapy. She noticed there was a down side to this procedure, even though it might help. She found books written by women who had essentially transcended their physical imbalances by moving into a deep place of introspection and understanding. She realized that there are many levels to consider. Perhaps with a little trial and error she would be able to make her own path through this new territory.

Mary decided that what she needed to focus on was the "pause" part of menopause. From her reading, she realized that this is a time for women to move inward and take stock of their previous life, their passions, their gifts and ponder who they want be when this passage is complete. Mary decided to give herself some space to meditate on this. Thus the intention was identified.

She then moved into exploring the idea. Would this mean silence? Could she do this alone? Would she like company? Did she need to go away? What kind of environment would support her mission? Did she need a professional to help her along the way?

When enough questions were asked, she moved into action as the plan became clear. Mary would design a long weekend. She would ask three special friends who were also facing menopausal issues and were of a like mind to join her. In the designing, she would ask each woman what she needed for the weekend and thus the plans would emerge. They would share food preparation, as they would retreat to a friend's cabin in the mountains. Silence mixed with sharing time would incubate the interior processing.

Mary was marking part of the menopausal journey by honoring her changes and those of her friends. Since their experiences and needs were all a bit different, they would share in the vision of what each wanted to happen during the weekend. The specific and the collective were respected.

Before leaving on their retreat, Mary found four lovely small glass goddesses in a local store. She bought them to give to herself and her friends as offerings to remind them of their sacred journeys. This little taliswoman would be their guide as they finished the rest of the road to wholeness, which emerges after the menopause experience.

By embracing the concepts and changes, these women would be able to begin to understand what was happening to them, reach deeply into their hearts for closure from their previous life of childbearing years, and regard the shift into the role of elder as a natural process.

In our youth-worshiping culture, we women of a certain age need to step up to the plate to recreate the images of ageing. Mary saw that she wanted to be part of this transformational opportunity. Her choices in honoring this menopausal time gave her some tools and knowledge to move forward.

Elizabeth experienced menopausal symptoms for about eight years. The various signs would ebb and flow depending on what was happening in her life, what she was eating, stresses and other variables. She finally decided to step into the scene and embrace it, rather than feel a victim of this change of life. By adjusting her attitude, her entire experience shifted. Here is one of the things she did to honor what was happening to her.

Transformation

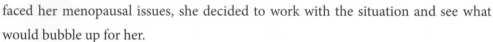

Elizabeth has a dramatic streak in her and loves to play, create, and move. As she faced her menopausal issues, she decided to work with the situation and see what would bubble up for her.

Elizabeth was aware of the messages that came monthly at the onset of her menstruation time—PMS issues that needed to be dealt with. She and many of her friends realized that they were vulnerable during this time. The faces they put on for the world for the rest of the month didn't work. They would get irritable and grouchy about things they would ignore at other times. What did that actually mean for them? Elizabeth began to notice that if she didn't acknowledge these issues, they would temporarily disappear, only to resurface. This emotional baggage needed to be identified and then sorted out. Elizabeth wondered if menopause acted as the last hurrah for the monthly information offered by her body? If she would take the time now to meet her demons, would she be lighter, more loving and ready to move into the rest of her life? She decided that she would take this path of exploration and see where it would lead her.

Elizabeth realized that she needed time and a plan to undertake this big project. It was a work in progress rather than something that could be fixed over a weekend.

She knew she was in for the long haul. She read books that gave her ideas about the journey that other women had taken during their transition time. She started to see some patterns emerge from the various writings. At first, symptoms would escalate to try to grab your attention. When you finally decided to notice them, you could manage them with drugs, or you could look your unfinished emotional business straight in the face and begin to focus on parts of life that been not working. Sometimes women needed a combination—some relief from symptoms so they would be able to look at the deeper issues.

Elizabeth found herself at the point where she had identified the work that she needed to do. She developed a plan to help her immerse herself in the hard stuff.

She found a therapist who could assist her. She started to write in her journal on a daily basis, noticing what would trigger her. She spent time looking into herself to reach the core of her problem issues. Instead of being as socially active as she had been, she used her available time to be more quiet, restful and introspective. She took a couple of weekends away from her family to sort things out. Her behavior changed and stumped her husband at first, but as he grew to understand her courage, he supported her.

Instinctively Elizabeth knew that a transformation was taking place. She had moved into her cocoon phase. She had put a protective shell around herself as she paid attention to her personal challenges. Even though she was still a wife, mom and employed, her discretional time was redirected to allow her the opportunity to process what she needed to do. She knew when she was done that she would be a stronger and freer woman, ready for the next phase of her life.

After several years, Elizabeth was ready to emerge from her cocoon—her self-induced period of personal discovery. She loved the image of the butterfly—the color, the ease of flying, and the change from caterpillar to a glorious new essence, the grace. She decided to design a transformation celebration for herself, as she was ready to present her new self to the world.

Since the journey took such a long time, there was no need to rush the celebration. Elizabeth waited for summer, when she and her friends could be outside—where butterflies live. She invited twelve of her closest friends and family members who would understand what she was doing. Not everyone in her life would be sympathetic to this unusual gathering. She designed an extravagant robe made from colored silk and other flowing fabrics that looked like a butterfly. She also found an old long white bathrobe, which would act as a cocoon.

When her friends arrived at the appointed place and time, Elizabeth was wearing her old bathrobe. There was a circle of blankets and chairs around a centering space filled with flowers. Each place had a note with a mission described on it. Go into the garden and collect a bouquet of what's available. Lie down flat on your back and look at the sky. Find twelve different colors of green in the area and bring back samples of them. Find four new smells that you haven't smelled before. Make a sketch with this paper and pen. Weave a wreath from the provided flowers. Each mission was different. When everyone had gathered, a bell rang to start the assignment with half an hour to accomplish the task—in silence.

The guests returned at the sound of bell where Elizabeth was still in her old robe in the center of the circle. She told her version of the story of transformation that was happening to her. She mentioned that it wasn't yet finished—more would be revealed—but she was rejoicing in the progress she had made. She unwound herself from the old robe and stepped out in the light with her beautiful new and colorful garment.

She then invited each woman to tell about the activity that she had just finished. What had she done? What had she observed? Did she see, smell, hear or feel anything new? The stories from each turned out to be a treasure for everyone. Taking that time out of everyday life to look at the world with new eyes was refreshing. By having a hands-on task to accomplish, the women were taken to a realm of reexamination, to re-evaluate the place of human kind in nature. Elizabeth gave her friends a gift of experience, so they might be more in touch with the road to discovery.

At the end of the afternoon, high tea was served. Real teacups and little cakes topped off an insightful afternoon. Elizabeth felt upheld as she wrapped herself around the concept being becoming a wiser woman—ready to tackle issues of injustice, suffering, and whatever else the Universe would to put before her. At the same time her heart was open for fun and deepening relationships.

After reading these stories, you understand the importance of honoring some of life's unusual passages. I hope your scope of visualization and dreaming has expanded. When you come to a place in your life where you feel the nudge to make a significant change, tune into it and trust your intuition. Using the recipe for concrete direction and the stories for inspiration, you are ready to create something gratifying and worthwhile.

You now move into the Part III, which shows the many of the faces of death and dying. By taking a hard look at your intention during these difficult times, a plan will reveal itself. By embracing the experience with a loving attitude, you can transform these awkward and tough times into moments of beauty and compassion. Loving is the bottom line.

Part III: Endings:
Final Passages

Moving into this last section, you are now prepared to meet more challenging times in your life—losing loved ones forever. It is doubtful that anyone is actually ready for the death of a cherished person, yet you can begin to embrace possibilities for yourself, and for your dear ones, by being proactive and thinking ahead about options. Reading stories about what real people have already done in their lives can inspire you to perhaps make plans before you are gone, talk to your family about what they might want for their memorials, and even move into a place where you are creating new traditions—all this can be accomplished through intention, courage and love.

Many examples of meaningful memorials have been brought to my attention. I love the way people have merged the essence of the departed into a celebration. They are letting the deceased lead the way, despite the fact that they are already gone.

I invite each of you to be sensitive and aware when faced with tough times. You have tools to assist yourself, and others, when the need arises. Be brave and reach out to see what wonder will unfold.

Terminal Illness: Taking Time to Finish Earthly Business

Sometime in your life you will be faced with a friend, a loved one, or even yourself, who has been given a short time to live. These awkward moments can be ripe with opportunity if you can move into an intentional space of honoring this person and not be afraid to confront the unthinkable—that you will lose them. The following stories show what people have done to support and connect during this difficult time. You have the tools to help design an appropriate and meaningful action.

This story tells of a woman who connects with her loved one on a daily basis, even though she lives far away.

Letters to Uncle Norm

Lilly's Uncle Norm was dying. Their families had been very close all her growing-up years—the cousins were like brothers and sisters. Lilly moved to another state and had small children. She couldn't be with Norm in person during his hospice time. It was the first time that she could remember being in a position of losing a person close to her. She had no experience on how to handle this.

Lilly was frustrated about all the things she couldn't do for Norm during this final illness due to the distance issue. She needed to transform her thinking from what she couldn't do into what she could do. She finally decided she could write him a letter. In fact, she would write him every day. Lilly would send a little note of inspiration, or fill him in on daily family activities, something to let him know that she was thinking about him. Lilly felt as if they were communicating. She was doing the writing and he was doing the receiving. He knew that she was thinking about him every day, even though she couldn't be present during his last months.

Norm's wife received the letters in the mailbox at home, and she took them to Norm's bedside to read to him. Each letter became a special moment for them. They looked forward to hearing from Lilly and what she had to share with them: what the children were doing, how the garden was growing, how they all loved him, how they would miss him, how they would know that he was still with them after he departed this world, and much more.

Lilly was brave in sharing her thoughts with Norm—even some that most people don't talk about. Perhaps using the written word, and doing it on a daily basis, unlocked thoughts and insights that might not have otherwise been accessed and shared.

Even today, Lilly's heart is lightened when she thinks about those letters of connection. It was a proactive move on her part, not sitting around and waiting for something to happen. The intention was to find a way to let Norm know that she was thinking about him even though she was far away. This was before the days of email, which couldn't have done the same job anyway. Snail mail offers better communication for the heart—real handwriting and artwork with a personal touch. This correspondence, even though it was one-way, encouraged creativity on a daily basis. It was a fun challenge to come up with something new. Lilly doesn't ever remember that the commitment that she made for herself was a burden—a challenge, yes; a burden, no.

Here is an illustration of researching circumstances and personality to set up a lovely experience for a person in his last days. Everyone connected with George enjoyed the result of this creation.

George and the Birds

George was experiencing his last weeks under the care of his family and hospice. He had an attractive room with windows to an open yard. He was emotionally available for his visitors. He was still interested in life and all that was going on around him. His family decided they needed something to entertain George. From that clear intention and exploring options, the family decided to buy a bird feeder, which was placed just outside George's window. Many birds came to visit this feeder. No one in the family had been "birders" before. Almost everyone visiting George became entranced with the birds. Someone gave him a bird identification book. The birds provided constant entertainment as well as interesting conversation. Everyone, including George, was learning about the birds. He was connected to nature even though he was confined to his bed. The birds offered everyone pure pleasure. They brought beauty and nature in the midst of a painful situation.

I love this story. The intention was very clear to try to come up with something more for George—something he could relate to that wasn't physically demanding. The idea of the bird feeder was clever. It worked beautifully for this situation, offering healing and balance for all the participants. It offered release from the daily tedium that is often a part of a hospice experience. It presented a constant source for conversation. It was interesting to me that the feeder and birds were not a part of their lives before this time. The birds offered something fresh and new. Nature provided another magical miracle. George's family recognized the beauty and promise in that little bird feeder.

This proactive woman found a way to honor her dying brother. Because she included his local community, it was like a huge appreciation circle for a person who was going through a major health struggle.

A Celebration of Life

When her brother, Earl, was diagnosed with melanoma, Peggy thought a long time about what she would like to do for him — and for herself — to acknowledge this major life challenge. She had read the book *Tuesdays with Morrie* and was inspired by the concept of celebrating a life before it is gone. She talked with Earl about having a family reunion in his hometown. As part of the reunion, Peggy decided to organize a living memorial for Earl. He agreed to the idea and Peggy continued with her plans.

Peggy enlisted the aid of a close friend of Earl's, who lived in the vicinity and knew the local people who were important to him. He also helped find the venue and rent the hall for the gathering. The invitations were sent out.

Dear Friends,

As many of you know, for the last two years my brother, Earl, has been battling cancer. On the weekend of May 2-4 we're organizing a family reunion at the UBC conference center, and we invite you to a special "Tribute to Earl" from 1-3 on Saturday afternoon at the (place and address). This is our opportunity to show support for Earl and his wife by sharing poems, anecdotes, pictures, songs, etc. We're all hoping that the advance of the cancer can be reversed. Earl has been doing all that the medical establishment has suggested, and I believe that if we all send our healing thoughts and prayers to him it will help. Our 83-year-old mother will be attending from California, and of course, it will be comforting for her to know that Earl has such concerned and caring friends. Earl has shown great strength and courage as the illness has progressed, and I'm hoping you will share my need to show him that we love him. Please RSVP to. . . .

TRIBUTE
to
EARL
★
Please Come
• • •

Peggy wrote to me: "At the tribute, I played guitar and sang a couple of songs. My cousin also played and sang. Lloyd, (Peggy's husband), and I made a photo display, which represented Earl's whole life, and other people brought photos, too. My other brother read a poem from a book Earl had written, which resulted in a couple of cousins wanting copies of it. In April, Earl let himself be talked into going to a faith healer in the Philippines, so the tribute included a very interesting telling of that story, which Earl had intended to write, but hadn't. I had booked the hall for two hours, but people stayed around and visited longer. I didn't want it to go too long because I was afraid both Mom and Earl would get tired."

I was touched when I read this story. The courage comes in two forms: Peggy for stepping out to offer an unusual gathering, and Earl for being able to receive it. The inspiration comes from hearing the story of what one family has chosen to do when challenged with change and illness. The healing came for Peggy because she was able to find some way to do something to honor her brother and his journey. The healing may affect Earl by knowing that he is loved, and that love has been expressed in spite of whatever may happen to him with the cancer. These are not easy issues to face squarely. This family has done so with dignity and sensitivity.

A family found a way to bring part of an island home to the city. Instead of totally missing her previous life, a dying woman was surrounded with many places she loved. Every time her eyes opened, she was reminded of a happy site.

The Love Wall

Gloria was in the late stages of Parkinson's disease. Her family decided she needed to move from her beautiful home on an island in Puget Sound to Seattle, where she was closer to medical care and relatives. This was a huge shift for her and she missed the beauty that she had out her window on the island.

Gloria's friends and family put their heads together to try to devise something that would help her enjoy what time she had left, even if she was bedridden and in town. They thought about what was important to her: her island-view and home, her family and her friends.

What emerged was a lovely plan to transform the room into a haven of peace and beauty. On the wall to Gloria's left, the family had taken pictures of the island and the view from Gloria's house, which they blew up to a large size. They attached these photos to the wall, so when she wanted to see her former home, it was right there.

At the end of the bed, they constructed an ancestor alter. Pictures of Gloria's grandparents, parents, family members who had passed on were placed there watching over her and connecting her to her lineage.

To the right, the wall was filled with pictures of friends and people dear to her. Loved ones and beauty always surrounded her. These scenes and pictures gave her great comfort when she couldn't leave her bed. She was never alone. The love of those around her kept up her spirits when she was passing through difficult times.

With some exploration and using their creativity, Gloria's friends came up with this unusual mural idea to envelop her with soothing beauty to keep her company. Such simple inspiration made a big difference to this woman who was feeling somewhat alone and distant from her home. It didn't take much money, but it took some gathering of materials and offered a powerful picture of comfort for Gloria.

This is a precious story about a woman who found a way to connect with her very sick sister. Many hands contributing to this heartfelt project make it especially moving.

A Thousand Cranes

Sally's sister, Nelle, was diagnosed with an aggressive cancer. Sally lived in the West and Nelle lived in Florida. The long distance was a frustration for Sally. She talked often with Nelle and the two decided on a plan of action to see each other. Meanwhile, Sally felt she wanted to do something to acknowledge Nelle and connect with her in some way other than the phone.

Sally is an art teacher at the middle school and sees many children during the school day. For one of the art projects, Sally decided to help the kids learn to make origami peace cranes. These little cranes are lightweight, beautiful in design, and full of color and movement. Sally decided to ask the students, and anyone else who wanted to participate, to help her make a mobile of a thousand cranes to send to her sister. Imagine the love, concern and best wishes going into this project when all the crane makers knew they were making them to send to this woman facing a life-threatening condition.

Sally hadn't told Nelle about this project. It didn't take long to finish the mobile and send it off. Nelle was overwhelmed and delighted with this group of people, most of whom she didn't know, working together to make her this amazing piece of art. She hung it over her bed as she dealt with her treatment.

As it turned out, Nelle died unexpectedly just the week before Sally was to arrive for her visit. The cranes had flown across the miles and offered a connection. Whenever Nelle had looked them, she knew that Sally was with her in spirit.

Loss of Animal Friends: Letting Go of Favorite Pets

If this topic seems trivial, you don't have to read this chapter. Yet many people spend time, energy, love and money on the animals who live with them. For some, they are as much family as the humans in their lives. To many, the animals offer more unconditional love and attention than any person. When one of these beings leaves, a gaping hole remains in the heart. You are thought to be a little strange to have a huge memorial for your pet, yet somehow, many people need a way to honor this being and process the passing. I am including some stories telling how people have created meaningful moments to pay tribute to their animal friends.

This story helps you to realize that giving yourself permission to be sad and design some sort of commemoration when your pet dies can help the empty heart.

Bella's Space

Bella was our dog—a Husky-mix picked up at the pound as a puppy about twelve years earlier. Our family had many adventures during her time with us. My husband and I were going on a trip, so we had made arrangements for her to stay with our daughter who lives five hours away. Bella had a good day on Friday, going for a bouncy walk. That evening, she had a massive stroke. Our daughter, Melissa, called wanting to know what to do; the dog's condition was terminal. We knew it was time to release her from this world. Melissa took Bella to the vet, and he let her spirit go. As Melissa brought the body back to her house to bury her in the yard, there was a full double rainbow over the road. Through her tears, Melissa's heart smiled. She knew Bella was connecting with her as she left us.

Meanwhile at home, as we hadn't left yet, I couldn't stop crying. Anyone who called got a tear-ravaged voice on the phone. Bella's death came so far from me, and my husband was not home at the time of the call. I needed some concrete way to honor her. A bit on the spontaneous side, I felt I wanted some symbols of Bella with me for a while. I set up a little table in the family room. I found several pictures of our family and Bella to put on the table. I added a candle, as I needed something bright and alive to feel her spirit attach with mine. I found a small bouquet of flowers and one of her dog collars. For a week or so, I could be with Bella through this little altar. Her memories would move my heart as I was reminded of her constantly.

I didn't know what to do during this time. My tears needed physical expression, and the little table is what manifested itself. I needed a place to look at and hold the memories, the joys and the sense of loss. This was a private time for me. I was creating the meaningful moments to help me believe that Bella was gone and would never be home. For me, this little action bridged the gap from life to death. A friend brought over a flowering dogwood tree to plant in our yard to remember Bella. When I see this tree each day, part of Bella is still here.

Another simple story tells about remembering an animal friend.

Else's Candle

Else the dog left this world after a close and long contact with Angie, who doted on her. Angie and her husband have no children, so their animals take on an even more special place in their lives. When Else died, Angie said she lit a simple candle for her. The candle stayed lit for many days until it was done. Angie said that the light and flame helped her feel Else's spirit moving to another place. It connected them on Else's journey. This is not an elaborate ceremony, yet it reflected what Angie needed to do to create something to pay tribute to Else.

Recently I mentioned to Angie that I had put this story in the book and she shook her head, remembering the power of that light. Even though it had been several years since Else's passing, Angie recalled that the candle had been very meaningful for her at that time

Last year as I was planting some new rhododendrons on the property line between our house and Angie's place, I found one called Else. I chose that plant and it now holds the space for Else's memories, especially in the spring when the spectacular flowers show up.

Sometimes what you create doesn't have to be elaborate or public. You can search your soul for the guidance to do what is right for you at this moment. When you have an intention and know your animal, you will be able to design a meaningful moment that honors the relationship you had with your pet. Please trust that this can happen. Understand that this honoring is part of your personal processing package that begins mending your heart.

This impromptu ritual harkens back to ancient practices of helping the departed be prepared for their next life.

A Final Resting Place for Blaze

Blaze was a horse that had lived with Nan and her family for more than thirty-five years. One day, Nan found him peacefully dead in his paddock of natural causes. He had moved with Nan across the entire country—from Connecticut to Washington—about twenty-five years earlier. He helped Nan and her husband raise their children. They spent many happy years together.

Of course, Nan knew that the day would come when Blaze would leave them. Even though she knew it was going to happen, the reality of it caught her a bit by surprise. She had planned for him to be buried on their property, so that decision was made. Nan's husband dug a huge hole for him with a backhoe. Blaze slid into his final resting place very easily and comfortably. Nan decided she wanted to send him to his new pastures with everything he might need. She put his feed bucket, halter, grain, and some hay in beside

213

him. She then proceeded to talk about their shared history—thirty years of memories. Nan and her husband were the only people present. Both of them were in tears as they remembered the stories of Blaze and witnessed for each other his special place in their lives.

Afterwards, Nan wrote a long letter to each of her children talking about Blaze. She sent photos to remember this horse. She told the stories again in her journal, so they wouldn't get lost.

Nan felt that this ceremony/funeral/ritual was exactly what was needed for her to honor her animal friend. She was filled with grief at the loss of her horse, yet was able to begin the process of letting him go and moving on with her own life, because she had taken time, effort, and energy to acknowledge him.

Miscarriages: Remembering Those Little Souls

An area of loss not often acknowledged in American culture is that of a child through miscarriage. The American Pregnancy Association estimates that nearly three million unborn children die each year in the U.S.—over one million fetuses are lost due to natural causes. The dreams of the parents for this child are very real. The grief can be overwhelming. When you don't have a way to process this loss, you can be adding extra emotional baggage, which stays longer than is helpful and healthy. When you can create an acknowledgment of the loss, create a place and time to grieve and cry, perhaps with people who will share your journey, you can then begin the road to moving forward in your life. Your experiences will always be with you. How you choose to work with them makes the difference later on. I am grateful for the people who have been willing to share their stories of miscarriages and what they have done to honor the experience. I am hopeful that they will also help you, if you have been through this kind of loss. It is not too late to process what happened long ago. Reach deeply into your own heart and you will know what you need to create for yourself, your baby and life partner, to honor this unexpected and difficult time.

The demonstration of previously unexpressed grief finally allowed this young woman to look at her loss and thus be better prepared to receive her new child.

Kate's Story

Kate had waited a long time to get pregnant. First of all, her husband wasn't ready to have children. That took about five years. Then it took another year and a half to finally get pregnant. They were excited and thrilled for this new being to be a part of their lives.

When, at about three months, Kate began to bleed heavily, she realized that something was wrong. She miscarried. Life went on as best it could after experiencing such a loss. When the first year anniversary of the event came round, Kate began to notice certain feelings coming to her—remembering the pregnancy and the dreams surrounding that baby and their life together. At that time, she made a conscious decision to commemorate the date of the loss. The time had come to acknowledge the grief, which was still locked inside of her.

A poem poured out of Kate a couple of days before the actual anniversary date. She and her husband decided to go to the beach, as they wanted to send out a remembrance of this child into the sea. Kate felt attached to water. The baby was living in fluid and died in fluid. The water and ocean were symbolic to all of them.

The couple went to the beach on the evening of the anniversary. They read the poem. There was an amazing sunset charged with huge storm clouds. A double rainbow with two seagulls flying through it added to the already beautiful scene. The plan had been to weave a wreath of something from the beach, and to release it back into the ocean to honor the child. The reality was that they were overcome by the demonstration of nature. Kate found herself crying as she had never cried before. The tears and grief seemed to be coming from a place so deep she didn't know it existed. With the release came a sense of peace, as the grief was finally allowed to penetrate the world and leave her body.

They found a piece of seaweed and let it float away in the gentle waves. They

laughed, as the wreath didn't materialize, yet the seaweed made its statement. The change of plans lightened to the scene and appealed to their sense of humor, which was needed at that moment.

This time of honoring the anniversary of the passing of their child assisted them on the road to acceptance, processing still existing grief and opening them for the joy of their next baby, as Kate was again pregnant.

There is a wonderful ebb and flow of intention and letting go in this story. The intention, with a shell of a structure, allowed the process to begin to unfold. The couple was then able to let the forces of nature come to their aid and assist them in healing.

The next story gives some practical ideas to help friends who are experiencing the loss of a baby, as well as what the couple did for themselves to acknowledge their grief.

Angel Baby

Don and Brenda lost their first child through miscarriage. Disappointment, failure, sadness and anger settled in their hearts. They had only each other for processing their grief. Several reasons kept them from the comfort of their family and friends during this difficult time. Few windows of opportunity to tell their story opened from their circle of friends. Family members lived far away. People were unable to talk with them about the loss. Miscarriage is infrequently discussed. In our culture, we don't have role models or training to know how to stand by others when they suffer through a miscarriage experience. Frustration compounded their already complex emotional state. A life-changing event happened, and the world didn't seem to notice. Furthermore, during Brenda's hospital stay, she found no emotional support from the staff, just clinical repair. Although the couple found a way through their grief, daily hugs from friends and family would have helped to lessen the sting.

Both Brenda and Don knew their emotions needed expression, and fortunately Brenda found two outlets for her feelings. During the pregnancy, the couple collected a few baby items, but Brenda wasn't clear what to do with them after the miscarriage. They talked about the hope that this child had brought to their lives. Brenda had the idea of saving these things in a hope chest to be available for a later time. They bought an unfinished chest, "sanded the heck out of it," painted it, and added an inscription on the inside that said, "I love you." The chest became the symbol of the lost child, as well as the dreams and hopes that came to them through her. Today the chest holds the toys of their two children. The spirit of the lost child, who they named Becky, seems to hover around it. The family feels her soft presence with them and she seems to be watching over them all.

219

The second outlet for Brenda came nearly five years after the hope chest. She found she was still holding grief inside of her that demanded expression. She turned to writing to see what emotions would emerge. A beautiful poem surfaced to commemorate the life and death of Becky and what she meant in their lives, but the anger was not gone. Brenda wrote, and wrote furiously, to reach the deepest places in her soul that needed expression. After an intense and cathartic ordeal with pen and paper, she finally felt the closure that she required to fully move on with her life and make her more available to her two beautiful children and husband. The gifts that baby Becky brought to their lives began to unfold. She will never be forgotten. Now she can rest gently in their family where her job is to act as the guardian angel to them all.

Brenda and Don were alone in their grief. Each person needs to figure out how to ask for help when the time comes when you can no longer handle your emotions by yourself. Ideally, family and friends can assist you during the tough times. This story underlines the fact that when friends and family are not available, individuals can create meaningful grief rituals to help the difficult times. Of course, being surrounded by a compassionate community may be the best way to work though the loss. Reading this story is hopefully a reminder to be sensitive and learn some skills so that constructive help is available when someone needs a friend to sit with them in troubling times.

Brenda, a professional child educator, helped me be aware of responses that are not useful. Some people may say that the couple can have another child, thus not taking the intenseness of this experience as seriously as needed. Others might mention that the fetus was only one month along, so it wasn't enough to fret about. They may say that the couple already has a child, so it isn't that bad to lose this one. One may think that there was something wrong with this baby and nature was removing the child, because she wasn't normal and healthy. Statistics show that nearly one half of all pregnancies end in natural termination. Brenda wasn't alone in her experience, yet that doesn't diminish the impact on her. The emotional grief of the couple is not being allowed to surface when they hear comments that don't support them to feel the full experience. Most people need to educate themselves to be sensitive and aware of the feelings that might surface when one loses a child.

What friends can do is:

 Acknowledge that the couple had a miscarriage and say you are sad to hear about it

 Ask what you can do to help the couple—it could be providing a dinner, taking a quiet walk with them, create a ceremony to honor the child, hold your friend so she can cry

 Let them know it is OK to be sad

- Offer to do errands with other children in the family
- Don't avoid them
- Write a note of comfort and support
- Offer to do some housework

Be sensitive and take initiative to assist your friends and family at this difficult hour. Anyone can learn the tools to support, love, and listen to those who need help. Be responsible and acquire some skills. Others will notice and this scenario will have a more satisfying ending.

This is a tough story about what might be. It makes me think about options in a difficult area of our lives. Most of us have been touched by miscarriage and/or abortion—either through our own experience or someone close to us. Often the question is, "How can I help myself or my loved one process this tragedy?" When we read about what happens in Japan, we may start to open our hearts for alternatives that might work to honor this passage. This is a work in progress and the intention is help people who have lost children to grieve, and then to begin to heal from the experience.

Unborn Children's Cemetery

In researching stories and information about miscarriages I was amazed to find out about customs in other cultures concerning unborn children. The one that really caught my attention is found in Japan. Apparently, Mizuku Jizo is a Bodhisattva (one who achieves enlightenment, but declines buddhahood until all other souls are similarly enlightened) who watches over miscarried, stillborn and aborted fetuses. As a result of his concern about them, Buddhist cemeteries for unborn babies abound all over Japan. Statues of small children adorn the cemeteries. Some of them are covered with hats and scarves to assist them on their journeys to the next world. I think the children are named as well. They have clothes so that Jizo can help them—their souls are sent to Purgatory, naked and scared. Jizo saves them in the sleeves of his robe and clothes them as he takes them to the next level of spiritual development. By doing so, he allows them to attain enlightenment—which is a big deal. Otherwise, they wouldn't have the chance to advance. And that's your Japanese deity story for the day. Here's a website that is pretty clear http://www.onmarkproductions.com/html/jizo1.shtml. This interpretation of Jizo is quite modern. The Japanese sort of made this up to deal with what we haven't yet.

What are we missing in our culture? Not that we need to have big cemeteries like those in Japan, yet can we incorporate another broader perspective on honoring our lost children? Could we actually implement a graceful and lovely place to pay tribute these little ones? What came to mind for me would be to have a wall in a cemetery dedicated to these children with a plaque inscribed with name and date. It wouldn't have to be very large; just a space for noting an important loss and having the experience acknowledged. A ceremony could go along with it.

Of course not everyone would want to participate in this ritual, yet those who are looking for and needing some sort of follow-up on their experience might finally have an outlet. Our culture can barely talk about miscarriage, let alone abortion. Normally we only hear about them when we might mention our personal experience, and suddenly stories come out of the woodwork that have been festering and unattended in the emotional crevices of the hearts of mothers, and also the fathers.

Preparing Your Own Funeral/Memorial Service

As I have been collecting stories about memorials and funerals, I have discovered people who have taken the step to create their own celebration prior to passing on. We all know we are going to die, so it is possible to be proactive and prepared. These examples are from folks who knew their death was imminent and were interested enough to design a plan.

This man knew what he wanted and went for it—no ifs, ands, or buts.

Do It Yourself

Frank was getting up in years. He was at a time in his life where he was thinking about leaving this Earth and about his memorial service. He had strong feelings about what he wanted to happen and not happen as people gathered to celebrate his life after he was gone. He realized that what he wanted was not necessarily in line with his family's tradition. He was the last of a staunch Episcopalian family. The remainder of this family moved into a fundamental Christian faith. He was afraid that if they planned his memorial without his direction, it would turn into what they wanted, not what he wanted.

Frank decided to take action and plan his own service. He met with the priest of his church to talk over options. He wrote up the entire memorial service, as he wanted it to be: hymns, scriptures, special music, all the parts that were important to him. He gave a copy to the priest at his church. He also filed a copy with his family lawyer. He now felt he could release that part of his future, knowing that it would be taken care of as he wished.

This is a story that I have heard several times on my quest for meaningful moments. More people seem to want to create their own memorial rather than let others design it. For many of us who lose a loved one, having the service already planned can lift a burden. If the terminally ill person has talked the plan over with the priest or his family members ahead of time, the service can flow easily, allowing the family and friends to use their energy in ways other than preparing the service as they move through the loss. Meaningful moments are created for both the departed and the family and friends who remain.

On short notice, this man created an ending experience for himself. Even though we all know we are going to die, sometimes the notice is shorter than expected. He didn't wait a minute, but followed his intuition to provide what he wanted for himself and his friends.

Celebrating Your Own Life

Mitchell found out on Thursday that his body was totally riddled with cancer. He was not given long to live. He was in pain at the time and somewhat weak of body, but not of spirit. He decided that he wanted to celebrate his life before he was gone. On the Tuesday evening following his diagnosis, his community helped Mitchell throw a big party. There was to be lots of music, as Mitchell was an incredible musician.

Eight cases of wine came from his personal wine cellar, as he said he wasn't going to be around to enjoy it. There was lovely catered food. People said their goodbyes to Mitchell and enjoyed being a part of the community spirit, which had upheld him over the years.

On Wednesday evening, the musical folks gathered in force to offer a musical tribute to Mitchell as a farewell. A full string orchestra played some of his favorite pieces. A friend acted as emcee and told anecdotes about Mitchell's life, interspersed with jokes. Several other community members presented more music and applauded the ways Mitchell had added his spirit, energy, and financial backing to enhance their town. Nearly five hundred people showed up to honor Mitchell at this unusual and heartfelt occasion.

As terrible as Mitchell felt, he came onto the stage and thanked everyone for being there. He said it wasn't he who did all these things, but that the group of people who lived in this town had inspired him and helped to make things happen. He asked the lighting people to turn on the house lights so everyone could see each other, as that was what all this was about—not him. With his last breath he embraced life as death was approaching, and he honored all who knew him.

He died the next evening.

Here was a man who made a conscious decision, on short notice, to celebrate with his friends before passing on. He marked the moment for himself, as well as his family and friends. Many people weren't comfortable with this concept, yet others felt he was setting a new model. Bottom line: it didn't matter what anyone thought, as Mitchell chose what he wanted to do, and it was perfect for him.

This woman was interested in a plain departure box to get her to the crematorium. From that request her family added their embellishments.

Home Funeral

Lizzie Peacock was dying and she knew it. Her time wasn't far away, so she was making plans with her family for what would happen to her body after she passed. She wanted to be cremated. Her son built her a lovely wooden box that would take her body to the crematorium.

When Lizzie saw the beautiful box, she told her son to save the wood and use it for another purpose. It was much too fine a piece to burn up. All she wanted was a

229

cardboard box.

After Lizzie died, she was put into her cardboard box. Friends and family gathered to prepare to send her on her way. An artist friend painted a peacock on the outside of the box with big, fancy feathers. People who came to the home funeral were given the opportunity to color in the feathers. They also brought pictures of themselves to tape inside the box, so Lizzie wouldn't be alone. Each person was also asked to put a tracing of her hand on the outside of the box. The hands symbolized holding Lizzie up as she moved from this earthly life to the next.

This lovely tribute was designed by Lizzie and the family to meet their needs. The unique celebration felt just right for those attending and gave the final goodbye to one of their own.

When she passed on, this woman had already picked out gifts for her family and friends. It was a unique way to leave her mark with those she loved.

Recycle

Mary was a grand lady in our community. I met her years ago when our violin students played annually at a local gathering she hosted during the holiday season. She sang in the local chorale and was a member of the Daughters of Norway. She had a welcoming smile for everyone. I was so impressed when I heard what she wanted at her memorial service that I want to include it.

The first piece of the story begins on the day I went to our small, local Post Office and saw Mary's death notice posted on the wall. In tiny writing under the service information, a reminder had been added—Wear Purple. This immediately caught my attention and helped me think about Mary.

Later, I heard that a large table was set up in the church narthex at her memorial service. It was filled with objects from Mary's home, and everyone was invited to take one of these treasures to remind them of her.

The wearing of purple and the recycling of Mary's treasures are two small details, but they both touched me deeply. My guess is that Mary was the designer of both of them. She wanted the purple, and she wanted to give gifts to those who came to honor her. She had most likely picked them out, so they were ready when the time came. She was that kind of person.

This demonstration is unique in my experience. Before she passed on, Mary had planned a meaningful time for her friends and family. Her personality came through because of her requests and added her own personal touch to the memorial service.

Memorials and Funerals: Remembering the Uniqueness of the Departed

Death takes our loved ones from us. One way or another we try to believe that the departed are all right, wherever they are. We, who are left behind, are the ones who mourn, express our grief, and need to continue with our own lives. Acknowledging these losses can be a profound and deeply meaningful time if we allow ourselves to feel the experience. The healing process can begin through intentional recognition of this passage.

Memorial services, a time when the departed is honored, are common in today's American culture. Honoring can have many styles. I would like to suggest that those of us venturing on the journey of paying tribute to a loved one be prepared to embrace this opportunity. This is when we can present the personality, life, and essence of our special person. We can learn about our loved one in a new way if we take the time to prepare her story.

The woman in our next story found an unusual way to honor her husband and keep a very personal reminder of him with her.

Memorial Quilt

Rosa's husband of forty-three years had recently died. She needed to go through the closets and remove his personal belongings. She had a difficult time dumping these items, which she had looked at and that had been a part of her life as well as his.

Rosa was a quilter and a seamstress. She decided that she would make a quilt to remember and commemorate her husband and their time together. She identified special times in their life—when and how they met, their wedding, their children, special vacations, vocational memories. She cut up his old clothes and introduced them into a quilt. She lovingly recreated their life using what was left. His suits made up the square about his professional life. His golf shorts and shirts made the sport square. She created a work of art and a meaningful moment from what might have been a difficult and wasteful task—getting rid of his clothing

The next story tells of a man given a mission, which he accepted, but was unable to perform immediately. It shows how it is OK to forge your own path when issues of the heart are involved.

Ashes on the Mountain

Brad's sister died in a tragic car accident when she was thirty-four years old. The family was distraught and full of grief when they lost Carrie. She had been an extremely active, outdoorsy sort of woman. She hiked, loved the mountains and backpacked. After her body was cremated and put into a small wooden box, Brad was given, and accepted, the mission to spread Carrie's ashes from the top of one of her favorite mountain peaks. He took the box and made the long and strenuous climb to the top. The day he made the trip was clear and beautiful, where he had a 360-degree view from the peak. When it came time to open the box and let the ashes blow free, Brad couldn't do it. He was not ready to let her go. Instead he found a tree off the trail, which had a wonderful deep crotch in it. He settled the box into

235

the notch and returned home. He told no one that he hadn't tossed the ashes in the wind. A year-and-a-half later, Brad was ready to do his job with the ashes. He made that big climb again and found the obscure tree. The box had been perfectly protected. He retrieved the ashes, opened the box and was able to let them blow free on this trip.

This is a lovely story of the intention of spreading Carrie's ashes. The family decided on the site and commissioned Brad to carry out the plan. The last piece of the formula is to let go of the outcome. When Brad got to the top of the mountain, he was not able to free the ashes. He was able to recognize his inner guidance, which told him to wait for more appropriate timing. By letting go of the desired outcome—the expectation of letting the ashes go—Brad was not tied into the pre-made plan. The ending of the story was not as anticipated, but it turned out to be the right one anyway.

A unique story unfolds as a woman searches for a way to keep her son's memory with her in an unusual way. She finds expression for her need and acts on it.

Darren's Doll

Darren died suddenly at age twenty-one of natural causes. After some time had passed, Martha, his mom, felt as if she needed some physical representation of him in her daily life. The intention was clear—she wanted a reminder that he was with her every day. Martha spent some time thinking about this, and was eventually guided to an artist she knew who was skilled in designing dolls and representations of a spiritual nature. Martha contacted him with her wish, asking if he would be able to assist her in creating something that she and various family members could keep with them in their pockets or purses. She had been inspired by the old Russian folktale of Vasilisa, where the daughter carries a doll that represents her mother's spirit. In this case it would represent Darren's spirit. Martha wanted five of these dolls.

The artist seemed honored to be part of this process of creating a symbol for Martha. His initial idea was to use a small clear glass bead for the head, like those used in flower arranging. A picture of Darren would be glued to the back of it and act as a magnifying glass. He designed a wooden body base in the shape of an arrowhead with Darren's head attached. Each body needed to be decorated by the person who was going to be keeping the symbol. As it turned out, the pieces were too big to be carried around, but were perfect to be kept in a place of honor in the various households where they would go.

This may turn out to be a long project for Martha, as she found herself not yet done with processing the death and there is no time limit. Down the line, a smaller version of Darren may emerge—one to be carried around as originally planned. The doll idea is taking on a life of its own and will materialize when it is ready, especially because Martha keeps her clear intention.

The letting-go piece of this story is interesting. Martha didn't allow the larger doll to disappoint her just because it didn't fit into her purse. She seemed to understand that perhaps Darren wasn't yet ready to travel in a small place. She invited the Universe to show her a broader picture of her intention and stay with it until it is ready to manifest itself. This story is not concluded—more will come to Martha when the time is right.

This is my story of trying to figure out how to honor my sister at a family gathering when we placed her ashes in the columbarium. The idea that emerged is a little different, but worked for us.

Painted Toenails

Two-and-a-half years after my sister died, the memorial garden where her ashes were to be placed was finished. I wanted do to something special with the family. Carol was my only sister. She was well-groomed all the time. I especially admired her manicured toenails and fingernails, but mostly her toenails were awesome to me. Even when she died, her toenails were beautifully red. I didn't spend much time on nail grooming until after Carol died. Since that time, I've tried to keep my toes polished in honor of her. Every time I look at them, she is with me.

As I thought about creating something meaningful, my thoughts kept going back to her toes. I decided to invite Carol's two daughters, our mother, her mother-in-law and myself to have a pedicure before the service. This was how I wanted to honor Carol's memory. Meaningful moments don't have to be deep and intense. They can be whimsical and fun, even at a serious time like this. The five of us went to a salon and hung out together enjoying the camaraderie that women can build when being together. We held Carol in our hearts during that time. I knew she was smiling at our beautiful toenails as we slipped her ashes into their final resting place.

Even when we may want to create a meaningful moment, we are sometimes not able to do it. The timing may not work out. Our comfort level is challenged. Read this story of a woman with good intentions who couldn't move into action. Perhaps another time will present itself where she can resolve the unfinished business she carries with her loss.

Frustration

This story has a strange twist to it. As my husband and I walked to the door of a party given in December, the power went out. We entered into a darkened world. As soon as the candles appeared, so did the outlines of faces. It took some time until we could start to recognize our friends.

I met Connie at this party. We started talking. Her stepmother had just died. She told me about her step-mom and the relationships in the family. I could feel the sadness in Connie's heart. Also present was a sense of frustration that the funeral didn't sound like it would allow for any connecting time for the family members. We talked about various ideas where the family would be able to communicate on a more intimate level. The formal church service didn't sound like it was going to offer a personal touch. In theory, she thought these suggestions sounded great. Then she said, "I don't think I can do this."

Connie is a bright, attractive, outgoing woman in her fifties. I was surprised at her response, yet glad that she felt she could be honest about it. I had planted the seeds and now needed to let go of the outcome.

A couple of weeks later, I was curious and wanted to know what happened. I called Connie. She said that she hadn't done it. She commented that the scenario just didn't turn out the way she had hoped. The funeral had taken place in the culturally accepted fashion. It was taken care of, even though she didn't have a sense of completion about the occasion.

I am including this story, as it is sometimes necessary to realize that plans may not come to fruition as one may hope. I was a vehicle to talk over options with Connie. She made the choice to act on the intention at this time or not. Perhaps the story isn't over yet, as she still harbors a sense of incompleteness. The seeds were planted and there may come another occasion where the opportunity to gather and talk with the family may happen. If not, so be it. This is part of the lesson of letting go.

This small story packs a big emotional punch as the community hears the symbolic passage of the years.

The Tolling Bell

A local church has a tradition at a memorial or funeral service to ring the bell the number of rings as the person was old. As the bell tolls, the guests are asked to think about the life of the deceased. When the bell rings at four, one might think about them learning to ride a bike. At eighteen, they would be going to college, getting a job or going off to war. When they are thirty, they have just had another child. At sixty, they have retired from a long career. This tolling of the years can give some perspective to the life and allow the guests to relive moments of their departed friend or relative.

When this church was new, they didn't yet have a big bell. They tried a little hand-rung bell or a gong. It didn't have the same impact as the big bell ringing the years into the community at large. There is something powerful about sharing the years through the tolling, which is healing and allows for contemplating the loved one through the journey of life

A memorial service helps give closure to the family of the departed. What happens when there isn't one? Read about a woman who struggles to find a means to honor her loved one when there was no formal gathering.

Unfinished Processing

Susie's mom died wanting no memorial service or funeral. Her only direction was that her body be placed alongside her mother in the family plot in Ohio. Susie and her three brothers took care of that last wish. Yet deep in her heart, Susie was unable to let go of her so easily. Susie was a priest herself and closely related to the healing that can come with a witnessed celebration of the departed. She finally realized that she needed to create something to help her grief process to unfold.

As Susie thought about what she needed, several ideas came forth. At first, she sat down with family photos of her mom. As she looked at them, Susie would consciously release her mom from this world. She relived the memories that the photos invoked, and then let them go. This process was helpful, but it wasn't enough to allow closure.

At a later time, Susie met with a priest friend and his wife to design a requiem mass for her mom. Susie felt she needed witnesses with her, yet it didn't need to be a big production. Her friends sat at a kitchen table set for a Eucharist and had a lovely service for her mom. Part of the service included Susie talking about mom. She talked for nearly an hour about this person who had birthed and raised her, about their relationship, about Susie's views of her as a person. This service allowed for another step for closure for Susie.

As Susie was recounting this story to me, tears and grief reappeared. What she found out by revisiting the story of letting her mom go was that her mom's absence wasn't quite fully processed. In this case, Susie may need to continue to look for more ways to connect with her mom and to move through the grieving and then letting go. More meaningful moments may appear as this story fully unfolds and ultimately reaches a closure.

★

When my dad died, we looked to him when designing the memorial. By taking his lead the service unfolded in a magical way that left everyone feeling satisfied.

Poems and Candles for Clifford

My dad, Clifford, died on December 1. He had been in poor health, but not dying. He became ill, went to the hospital, and lingered long enough that his close family could be with him during his final hours.

The principals in the family met to decide what to do to honor Cliff's passage and to acknowledge what we needed to do for ourselves. During this brief meeting, we decided on a memorial service to be held at Cliff's home church on December 6. Setting the date was a big decision in itself. Our intention was set and we could move on from there. My brother, Don, my mom and I were the ones to design what would happen for this service. We took some time to think, then gathered to review our ideas and options. One evening at my mom's house, we were reading from a book of poems that my dad had written and that my mom had collected. There were poems on his life philosophy, what God meant to him, about his granddaughters. There was our dad in his own voice right in front of our eyes. It was as if he was speaking from the next world through his writings.

My mom had definite ideas about what she wanted for a service—small and intimate, simple, at the church and have her family members play the music. When my brother had taken part of a night vigil with my dad before he died, Don had written ten things he wanted his two boys to remember about Grandpa. When he shared these with me, I cried and realized that Don had caught an essence of Dad that needed to be shared. It was as if Dad had been communicating with Don during their intimate hospice time. During the same night after Don left Dad's bedside, I stayed and read to him. He was on morphine, so although he was not communicating in words at that time, his presence was clearly felt. Toward the end of the night, a prayer came to me. Again it was as if Dad was funneling his words through me before he left. During that same night, I had a strong vision that we needed eighty-three votive candles at Dad's service. It was very clear that we needed to honor his eighty-three years of life. How they would be used was to unfold; yet I knew that I needed to include them in the memorial service.

Individually, the three of us brought our suggestions to our gathering time. We all felt that Dad had written part of his own service with his poetry. Together we picked several poems that covered various aspects of who Cliff was as a person. Don had captured the essence of Dad in his words to his children. I had written the closing prayer without even realizing it. We planned for the votive candles to be carried by the guests as they entered the church. Each person carried an unlit candle to the front of the sanctuary where they lit it and placed on the alter area. Cliff even inspired the flowers. He was an avid gardener and had lots of calla lilies in his yard. We were able to order a bouquet of calla lilies for the front of the church, which would be surrounded by the votive candles

After making these decisions and arranging the service in a loose format, we met with the minister of the church to collaborate with him. He seemed pleased with the work we had already done and added what he felt might be needed from his church point of view.

The service went off wonderfully. When all eighty-three candles were lit, it was a sight to behold. All the five granddaughters and I played violins and viola. My cousin plays the harp. The choice of music unfolded as we felt what was appropriate from Cliff's point of view. The harpist included Christmas carols in the prelude as well as "Take Me Out to the Ballgame" and a little nursery rhyme called "Pony Boy." We played his favorite tunes that he had heard through his time of being a parent and grandpa, supporting the musical life of us all.

After the service was finished, the congregation came forward and took a lighted candle with them as they left the church. Each person was invited to keep that candle to remember Cliff and the light his presence had put into the world. One grandson plays the drums. We asked him to play a cadence on his lone snare as people picked up their candles and walked out of the church, rather than a traditional postlude. By using this young man's talents, the closing of the service turned out to be quite dramatic.

This particular memorial turned out to be significant for all of us. By tuning into Cliff's being, and our own vision, the plan unfolded without effort. Even though it was a bit different, it worked. The process, and the service itself, helped us begin to move through our grief.

A wonderful postscript to this story came several weeks later. My mom received a note from a family who couldn't be present at the church service. I had told them when the service was going to be held and about the candles. At the same time we were in our church, this family was lighting their own candles and taking the time for each person to talk about what Cliff meant in their lives. They took a picture of them holding the candles and sent it to my mom. She was touched and felt connected to these people who couldn't be with us, but who took the time to honor Dad in their own way.

I like this story because the personality of the deceased is shared with a community who didn't know him. I think the guests felt as if they had a new best friend after attending this event, even though Jerry had already passed on.

Meeting Jerry After He Died

Jerry died in early January. He had one daughter named Lou. He had lived most of his life on the East Coast, moving only a year before his death to the West where Lou lived. He knew very few people in the area when he died. Lou wanted to plan a memorial service for him, even though it seemed a little unusual because so few people knew him.

Lou had two friends who offered to assist her with planning the service. As she was an only child and her mom had already passed away, she felt relieved that some friends wanted to help.

The three women spent a morning talking about Jerry—what kind of a person he was, what he liked, what he disliked, what his interests or passions were. Lou helped the two women learn about him. Notes were taken. The women asked Lou questions. Would he like a church service? Would she like a church service? Would they like a memorial outside, or elsewhere? The many questions helped Lou formalize what was important to both her and her father's memory.

This exploration part of the formula helped to design the service. They chose to have the service in Lou's church. Jerry loved music and especially organ music. The church had a great organist and a nice pipe organ. The music was left to the organist to choose, knowing that Jerry loved big organ and that he also loved hymn singing. Two hymns were picked for the service. Several family members from back East were asked if they wanted to write something about Jerry to be presented at the service. Several of them wrote vignettes about him. Lou herself wanted to talk about her dad. She had two favorite, appropriate scriptures that she wanted read. One of the women wrote a homily to connect living with dying—of his meaning in life as well as death. Jerry raised and loved roses. Roses were placed on the altar. He was an avid art collector, especially of triptychs. Lou brought a sample of his collection, which was also placed on the altar.

The exploration made the planning part easy. All the pieces were there, and one woman put them into a flow. The minister acted as host for the church. A "to do" list was made for Lou, so she could make sure all the chores were done before the service. Once Lou saw the flow of the program, she asked certain people to read and lead in the actual ceremony. She found great comfort in not being alone in designing the service

The planning of the service, as well as the service itself, turned out to be a part of Lou's healing. She trusted herself to pick and choose appropriate information about Jerry's life; she received support from her community of friends; she felt good about the service itself as being a tribute to Jerry and introduced him to a community who never knew the man.

This family designed a unique and appropriate time together where they interred the ashes of their dad. Inspiration led to a unique memento for each guest to take home as a reminder of the departed.

Bookmarking the Moment

Four concrete and marble walls, open at the corners so people could enter, encircled a small garden. Inscriptions filled one of the walls. Wrought iron castings for holding glass vases hung from the other three. Red roses and calla lilies filled the vases with a soft look and delicious smell adding life and color to the setting. Three backless benches made of wood and concrete snuggled into the courtyard. Out of one of the walls gushed and gurgled a fountain pouring its water into a cupped receptacle filled with smallish rocks to diffuse the spray. White azaleas and purple rhododendrons decorated the space with their jaunty flowers showing that all was well inside this safe and sacred place.

Slowly, thirty people—from grandparents to grandchildren—drifted into the columbarium. The hauntingly sweet music of strings filled the air with their soothing sounds. A square box sat on top of the inscription wall. Underneath it was an open space waiting to be filled.

A middle-aged woman glided forth to welcome the guests. Family and friends congregated to honor Alf, who was their friend, grandfather, dad, and husband. The box contained his ashes and was going to be placed in the opening in the wall.

A daughter-in-law stepped forth to read some scriptures. She had talked to her minister about passages for the occasion, but the decisions they made hadn't resonated with her. She needed to find new ones. She looked through her Bible and came across several readings that were perfect and captured Alf's essence. The words that have touched people's hearts for more than two thousand years could still convey the strength and generosity of this man. She followed her inner guidance to change the scriptures to meet her needs.

The son moved to center stage and took the box. He gently eased it into its final resting place. The sun began to push through the clouds, washing the group in light.

The daughter brought forward a bowl filled with strips of paper to hand out to each guest. Each laminated strip had a word on it that described Alf. Next to the word was a bit of artwork and colored ribbons floating off the ends. Each person read their word out loud and, if inspired, told stories about Alf triggered by their word.

CARS: Alf loved cars. He read the newspaper car classifieds daily. He kept up on the style changes, prices, good deals on used cars and would spend hours with anyone who would "talk cars" with him.

WSU (Washington State University): where Alf went to college. He used to tell stories of being a poor student at WSU in the Forties. He attended his fiftieth class reunion several years prior to passing. His son attended the same university.

GARDEN: Alf had a beautiful garden in his retirement home near the beach. He grew dahlias that lined the driveway going up to his house. They bloomed furiously every year with blazes of orange, red and white announcing late summer. Calla lilies multiplied like weeds. The rose bushes dazzled in the sun with more blossoms than leaves.

OPTIMISM: Alf suffered from rheumatoid arthritis since his late twenties. His chronic pain didn't interfere with his positive view of life, appreciating people, places, ideas, music and beauty, encouraging the rest of us to see it all as well.

The thirty guests shared "their" word about Alf. When the presentation was over, the group had a sense that Alf had been with them in a very real and tangible way. His being came back to life during these moments. Each guest took home the beribboned bookmark they had chosen as a reminder of this day.

The intention of this gathering was to honor Alf and put his ashes in their final resting place. His wife was clear about her requirements for the occasion.

- ★ She made a thoughtful guest list.
- ★ She wanted roses and calla lilies in the vases.
- ★ She wanted music played by her grandchildren.
- ★ She wanted the local pastor to participate.
- ★ She wanted her son to place the ashes in the wall.
- ★ She did not want guests to randomly speak about Alf or tell stories.

Her daughter explored options on what to do, and how to proceed with the celebration. She yearned for a personal connection with her dad during the ceremony. One night, the idea of the bookmarks emerged from the shadowy half-awake dreamtime. She went right to work to make a list of the descriptive words, used the computer to put them on paper, added the artwork, had them laminated, and added the colored ribbons. Somehow, deep down inside of her being, she knew that this way of paying tribute her dad, and connecting with the group, would be appropriate.

Because the exploration part was clear with the wife's leadership, the plan was easy. The wife found the site for the ashes, set the time and date. She sent out personal invitations. The daughter printed up a program that created a comfortable flow. The family knew what they wanted, put together a plan and then allowed it to unfold in natural way which included them all.

Our last story is sweet and simple, yet sends the guests away with a final wish from the departed and a guardian angel to keep an eye on them.

One Last Wish

Brenda's mom, Olga, had several shelves full of small porcelain, wooden and silver angels. Some she had bought for herself. Others she received from friends who knew about her collection, which began when her grandmother gave her the first one for her tenth birthday. Olga knew she had terminal cancer. She summoned Brenda to her bedside and asked her to give the angels away to friends and family after she was gone. Brenda's heart stuck in her throat. She was afraid, yet she understood the power of her mom's spirit reaching out to offer personal guardians to her loved ones. This gave Brenda the courage to act.

At the memorial service, Brenda stood by a table covered with her mother's angels and trusted that each person would pick a special favorite, knowing that her mom would be watching.

These difficult times of losing a loved one can have a silver lining when we allow the beloved departed to lead the way, be inspired by her life, to celebrate and take the best she offered and put it to good use. Recently, I was at a memorial where the departed was a difficult person. Rather than glossing over his thorny side, the family accepted that as part of who he was. He also had his redeeming side. By having the courage to celebrate both, his humanness was honored. We are all many faceted—that's what it is to be alive. We are connected, whether we consciously realize it or not. We learn from each other and grow from each other. Such is the beauty of life. When we can take these life lessons and respect them while honoring our departed, the richness they provide for those remaining is sprinkled throughout the universe. Our lives are fuller because of the ones who have gone before us.

Conclusion

You have now finished the first steps on an exploration that encourages you to become aware of events that might go unnoticed, yet have a big impact on your life. When you realize that you can embrace these significant times, they take on new meaning because you have intentionally decided to mark these moments as important. Recognizing these often overlooked opportunities begins the process of claiming them, which will add meaning to your life. By doing so, you may even experience opportunities of healing, satisfaction and grace.

Now that you have seen the recipe in action, you understand how it works in life. You can use it for any occasion that needs a bit of structure for organizational purposes. You can't do anything until you know what it is you want to do. The intention is so powerful that it leads the action. Pinpointing this initial piece of the puzzle is critical to the process of creation. It can be a fairly simple idea—plan a birth shower, honor a particular life transition, or celebrate the life of a person who has died. Even though these intentions don't sound earthshaking in themselves, you are clear about what you want to do.

The exploration part of the formula is fun because you look at different aspects of the person or event involved. You delve into their lives, their essence, their being, discovering in a new way what makes them who they are. Even if that person is yourself, you are seeing you with new eyes. It is this deeper glimpse of the person, with intention backing it up, that leads to what you need to know in order to precede. Asking at least twenty questions broadens the scope of understanding. The first questions will be fairly straightforward and easy. As you take the time to ask even more of them, you get to the interesting and challenging ones which will fine-tune your thinking.

With the exploration in place, the plan usually unfolds like magic. You see a pattern emerging, an angle appearing, or a theme developing. From that point, the ideas fall into place. You need to trust the process and let your imagination run rampant. Part of the charm of marking a moment is the creativity that materializes from you—with perhaps the help of some friends. You find yourself exploring directions previously unnoticed, and are unlocking joy, connection and meaning. Step into these sparkling shoes to dance your way into untapped places of sheer delight.

Conclusion

You will recognize that this process takes on a life of its own when it is initiated with love and honorable intention. When your inner critic tries to sabotage your plan with serious doubts, you will know in your heart that you are doing what you are called to do. The result may be a bit unconventional or quirky, yet allow yourself to bask in the event and let it speak for itself. You don't need to judge what has already manifested itself by your care and concern. Learn to accept the results and let them be.

By choosing to use the practices in *Celebrating Beginnings and Endings*, you have probably already realized that your life is changing. You see your friends with new understanding. You share heartfelt times of crisis because you know how to move into appropriate action. You set spaces for meaningful connection. You learn how to listen with your heart open to receive deeper messages from your family. The benefits arrive in unexpected places. You are in charge of making these occasions happen, because you have the tools wrapped in courage and creativity.

Don't be fearful to move ahead. Start with small steps to learn the techniques that will hold you when you are ready to tackle the more challenging times. There is nothing like appreciation to start the ball rolling—take a moment to show and tell a loved one how you value her. The results will open your heart to the possibilities of further explorations and build your trust in yourself. Using a friend for support is also a great way to spread the word of what you are doing and garner assistance for your planning. You are stepping into a place that may seem uncomfortable and unknown, yet when you reach into your deeper self, you will recognize that your innate wisdom and inner guidance understand how to do this. You just need an avenue of expression to help you retrieve what you already know.

We can help each other. It's through the stories of what we have all created that we find the incentive to move ahead with the next opportunity to mark a moment. We can connect on my website www.mark-the-moment.com or on my blog www.paulapugh.blogspot.com to share what we have crafted to help make this world a more compassionate place to reside. Together we can help establish a foundation for learning how to connect, communicate and listen to important people in our lives. Let's not wait any longer to get started. These messages are important and we are the messengers.

The next books to be published will include stories of annual events (holidays and birthdays), and relationships (family, work and community), and perhaps even an especially challenging one on tough times (mental illness, abortion, suicide). I would love to use your stories in these upcoming projects. If I use them, I will send you a free copy of the book in which it will be used. We need each other as we explore what is possible. Sharing is the best way to move down the path.

You now know you are on a path of no return. The benefits of creating significant occasions, where memories are made and stories share experiences, change your perceptions of yourself and others. In a world where conflict and greed run rampant, you have a means to shift energy. Take these tools and use your unique ability to focus your attention to honor the occasions that beg for notice. The small ripple that a pebble makes moves into larger circles and eventually merges with the ocean that connects us all. You are a part of the liquid circle of love.

About the Author

Paula Pugh lives on a Puget Sound Island with her two horses, dog and husband. After ending a twenty year career as a teacher, she launched into the next phase of her life: organizing women's health classes and retreats, and writing about making the most of meaningful moments in life.

Index

Notes